Dr. Carren Marvin

NUMBERS

WISDOM AS YOU WORSHIP

21st CENTURY CHRISTIAN

ISBN: 978-0-89098-898-5

©2023 by 21st Century Christian
Nashville, TN 37215
All rights reserved.

All rights reserved. No part of this publication may be reproduced, stored in a retrieval system,
or transmitted in any form or by any means—electronic, mechanical, photocopy, recording, digital, or otherwise—
without the written permission of the publisher.

Unless otherwise noted Scripture quotations are from the English Standard Version.

Scripture quotations are from The Holy Bible, English Standard Version® (ESV®),

copyright © 2001 by Crossway, a publishing ministry of Good News Publishers.

Used by permission. All rights reserved.

Cover design by Brent Bruce

DEDICATION

To Monkey,
whose heart of worship
has never faltered during the storm.
Love, Jane

ACKNOWLEDGEMENTS

This book was an emotional work, in that the COVID-19 pandemic happened right in the middle of my writing it. Like many, I felt the discouragement and isolation that came with what felt like an indomitable, endless, and devastating interruption to life as we knew it. It was hard for me to write because churches weren't even meeting in person. Ladies weren't meeting to study the Bible together, so what was the point of finishing *Numbers: Wisdom as You Worship?*

Several people saw the point, as it turns out, and encouraged me to continue. Providing much encouragement was my husband, Stephen, who is tireless in his support of me. My in-laws—Linda Marvin and Eric and Susan Marvin—were also enthusiastic about my writing, and this motivated me to keep going. I am also deeply thankful for my parents (Charles and Suzanne Green and Judy Green) and for my sisters and brother-in-laughter (Cherene Burley and Shea and Elizabeth Brock). We burned up the cell phone and Zoom lines during the pandemic, and the end result was always a stronger, more confident me.

I will always be thankful for the ministers and elders at Great Oaks church of Christ, especially for their relentless commitment to our congregation during the lengthy quarantines.

To the readers who have contacted me throughout the pandemic to share your enthusiasm for my books, God bless you. You encouraged me more than you know, and I pray you are blessed in your study of God's Word!

Last, but certainly not least, I am thankful for Stacey Owens, my editor at 21st Century Christian. Her enthusiasm for this project has never waned, even when the printing press was paused during COVID. She has a tireless attention to detail and style, and she offers her many edits with grace and kindness. What a blessing to work beside such a talented friend and sister in Christ!

"Let the words of my mouth and the meditation of my heart be acceptable in your sight, O Lord, my rock and my redeemer" (Psalm 19:14).

TABLE OF CONTENTS

Acknowledgements 4

Lesson 1: An Introduction to Worship 9

Lesson 2: Take Inventory 17

Lesson 3: Get to Work 29

Lesson 4: Make Sacrifices 43

Lesson 5: Stop Complaining 55

Lesson 6: Anticipate Heaven 65

Lesson 7: Watch Out 77

Lesson 8: Stay Hydrated 89

Lesson 9: Be Afraid 99

Lesson 10: Be Accountable 109

Lesson 11: Make the Time 119

Lesson 12: Clean House 131

Lesson 13: Leave an Inheritance 141

✢ LESSON 1 ✢

An Introduction to Worship

"'Hear, O Israel: The Lord our God, the Lord is one. And you shall love the Lord your God with all heart and with all your soul and with all your mind and with all your strength.'"

(Mark 12:29b-30)

Before you begin this lesson, answer the following questions.

In your own words, define *worship*.

_____

_____

Can you think of a person you've always admired—in Scripture or in your lifetime—for seeming to have a heart of worship? Who was that person, and what was different about that person?

_____

_____

In your own words, define *idolatry*.

_____

_____

What do you think some modern-day idols are?

_____

_____

Chapter 1: *An Introduction to Worship*

Part 1

If I asked a group of sincere, God-honoring church attenders what it means to **worship** God, my hunch is that most would immediately conjure an image of Sunday morning singing with fellow Christians. Certainly, that is a blessed, sweet opportunity we have each week to worship our Creator.

But is that it? We probably agree that it isn't. So what is worship when isn't singing? What does it look like? This is harder for most of us to explain.

My concern, however, is that if we are hazy on the details of what worship is outside our Sunday morning song service, then we're in trouble. I confess that paying attention to the words of the song and not to the cute new haircut my sister in Christ is sporting three pews ahead of me is difficult some Sundays.

Some Sundays...to be brutally honest...I am tired, and I am kind of hoping we skip verse 3 of the four-verse hymn.

Some Sundays, I'm annoyed that the song leader is standing too close to the microphone.

Some Sundays, I'm multitasking—singing while reading the order of worship and making mental notes of the baby showers, birthdays, or retreat dates that I need to add to my calendar.

Some Sundays, amazingly, I'm singing "Peace Like a River" yet simultaneously reading the riot act to my teenage sons if they don't stop laughing over the ear-numbing sneeze the man behind us just let loose.

Some Sundays, I'm wearing my church face and going through the motions because my husband and I argued that morning, and the kids waited until that very morning to tell me that their church shoes give them blisters.

Some Sundays, I'm just not into it.

Don't get me wrong. I don't underestimate the power of congregational singing each week. In fact, one reason I have come to love acapella worship is that all we hear is what God asks us for: our singing. I often cry ugly tears through our worship because that's what comes out when the peace of God moves into my heart. I absolutely love our times of singing, and, like you, I have my favorite songs—songs that remind me of my journey with God and Who He has been to me. Nothing is sweeter than these moments!

The painful reality, however, is that I am still a work in progress and, therefore, rarely manage to wholeheartedly focus on God for 100% of the song service. Even if I manage to do that someday in the future, though, that quantifies my worship to perhaps 15 minutes of an incredibly long week ahead.

That is, if **worship** is just about singing on Sunday mornings.

It can't be.

NUMBERS: Wisdom as You Worship

Read Job 1. Who was Job, and what was his reputation?

_____
_____

What was Job in the habit of doing, on behalf of his children?

_____
_____

Why would he do this?

_____
_____

In your own words, summarize the exchange between God and Satan.

_____
_____

What happens to Job's livestock, servants, and children?

_____
_____

What is Job's response to this unspeakable level of tragedy?

_____
_____

Revisit verse 20. How does Job put himself in a prostrate position before God?

_____
_____

How does Job's immediate subjugation to God challenge your typical response to trouble?

_____
_____

Chapter 1: *An Introduction to Worship*

Hear me on this: Worship CAN'T be the grand total of our singing on Sunday mornings. If it is, we are in hot water.

Big trouble, that is.

You see, every one of us spends more than 15 minutes of time loving on **something** (probably many things) during any given week. Every one of us gives 100% to **something** (probably something mundane) during any given week. Everyone of us gives our highest regard to **something** (probably something temporary) during any given week.

Which, when stacked against the quality and quantity of output we render during Sunday morning singing, leaves us guilty of a most egregious sin: **idolatry.**

Read Genesis 11:1-8. Whose greatness would the tower signify?

_____

_____

How does God feel about this?

_____

_____

What does God do in response to the people's self-glorification?

_____

_____

Idolatry.

Read any book in the Old Testament, and you can't miss God's biggest pet peeve. Actually, that's putting it mildly. On God's list of spiritual no-nos, this one is at the top. Even those who sleep through Leviticus still manage to categorically perceive idolatry as God's hot-button issue, one that is still a prevalent theme of the teachings of the early Church.

Before you sigh in relief, however, don't miss this topic's opportunity to bring a much-needed makeover to the hearts of 21st-century women. Maybe we can give an all-clear on handcrafted statues of foreign gods in our houses: The closest we get to a bronze Buddha is at the nail salon, and the only "statue" in our house is a Willow Tree rendering of a mother and child. With this survey, we can check idolatry off the list of sins to worry about, right?

Probably not.

NUMBERS: Wisdom as You Worship

Read Exodus 20:3-6. Make a list of the "shall not"s in these few verses.

_____

_____

Copy Exodus 20:23 on the space below.

_____

_____

Avoiding idolatry would be a piece of cake if all we had to look out for were marble busts of quasi gods. But you know, as do I, that the figurines are merely a focal point for the epicenter of our spiritual selves: **our hearts**.

For this reason, the topic of idolatry concerns everyone who has a pulse.

Part 2

At its core, the conundrum of idolatry is who and what we worship. But this is where we run into another broken fence: the one we try to put around our definition of **worship**.

If we could contain worship within the 15 minutes of congregational singing on Sunday mornings, then, once again, idolatry could be red-flagged with brazen confidence for any song that did not revere Yahweh, Jehovah God.

Read 1 Corinthians 10:6-11. What does Paul warn the church in Corinth against?

_____

_____

What seems to have been the outward expression of idol worship for the Israelites in Moses' day?

_____

_____

What does Colossians 3:5 equate with idolatry?

_____

_____

Chapter 1: *An Introduction to Worship*

Copy 1 Corinthians 10:14 in the space below:

_____

_____

Copy 1 John 5:21 in the space below:

_____

_____

The truth is that any "worship" that rises toward other "gods" is sin. One of the saddest moments in the Old Testament occurs when God—fed up with the Israelites' idolatry—encourages them to seek their deliverance from these inert, worthless gods. Yes, dear friends, even God has His limits. After delivering the Israelites time and time again, only to see them return to foreign gods e-v-e-r-y s-i-n-g-l-e t-i-m-e, God finally throws up His hands: "Yet you have forsaken me and served other gods; therefore, I will save you no more. Go and cry out to the gods whom you have chosen; let them save you in the time of your distress" (Judges 10:13-14).

I hurt for the children of Israel when I read these words. To their credit, they got rid of their idols once again, but the message from God was clear: If you want to worship these cultural icons, then you can pray for salvation in them, too.

This is where my hurt for the children of Israel meets my fear of the God of Israel. His message to me is no different, after all. **If I am going to profess Jesus Christ but bow to the icons of modern American culture, then He'll step back and let me see the kind of salvation that the world around me can bring.**

And it won't be pretty.

If I'm honest—perhaps more honest than you're comfortable with my being since I'm authoring a Bible study, of all things—some days I show off more pictures of my cats than I do glimpses of my faith.

If I may be so bold to say so, though, we all do it. Sports fans (especially in the South) wear their team colors, paint their faces, and cheer their hearts out for their favorite team. Netflix lovers charge their devices and shut out the world to binge watch their favorite series. Social media fans clock hours of screen time scrolling, posting, liking, tagging, and tweeting.

Holiday lovers go bonkers with decorations, costumes, cards, and foods—all to honor a day on the calendar. Black Friday shoppers embrace sheer madness among throngs of consumers, all suffering from a turkey coma but undeterred given what a huge sale any given big box store is having on TVs. Their determination to get one of the 500 said TVs may exceed their determination to get up for Bible class on Sunday mornings, even though Sunday School hours are more humane than Black Friday doorbusters.

Political enthusiasts follow every debate, post signs in their yards, and wave (or don't) the national flag—as if America were Canaan and this world were our home forever.

We can go on. Parents instill a love of cartoon characters in their children and spend dream vacations having breakfast with these famous icons. We spend endless hours at the ballpark or at the dance studio so that our children can play the game or make the squad. Modern parents run themselves into the ground hovering over their kids in the name of protection.

Our culture is a buffet of opportunities. Each one holds the potential to be a distraction-turned-idol.

Read Psalm 106:36-42. What happens when the Israelites started honoring the gods of neighboring cultures?

___

___

Read Judges 8:22-28. After subduing the land of Midian, Gideon and the Israelites make a trophy, of sorts. What becomes of this trophy, though (see verse 27)?

___

___

We have an urgent need for wisdom, knowledge, and understanding as we live lives as spiritual beings. Designed to praise and adore, we are prone to apply our affections to the competing interests of the world: sports, television, social media, holidays, nationalism, youth extracurricular activities, and so on.

James, the physical brother of Jesus and an apostle of the early Church, cautioned us that God, not surprisingly, "yearns jealously over the spirit that he has made to dwell in us" (James 4:5). God wants our worship, and He is rightfully jealous when we give it to someone or something else.

Read Jeremiah 48:7. Who is being worshiped in this idolatrous situation?

___

___

Chapter 1: *An Introduction to Worship*

Read Jeremiah 3:1. To what similar-sounding word is idolatry compared?

_____

Read 2 Kings 10:27. In Jehu's "zeal for the Lord" (vs. 16), he cunningly killed all the prophets of Baal. What did Jehu's men turn the house of Baal into? What does this tell us about how God sees idolatry?

_____

_____

The Book of Numbers comes with refreshing wisdom. More than dry census records inserted for historical reference, Numbers offers us the wisdom we need to sustain lives in worship of God and God alone. Consider God's central command to the Israelites, given through Moses, as they prepare to claim the Promised Land: "When you pass over the Jordan into the land of Canaan, then you shall drive out all the inhabitants of the land from before you and destroy all their figured stones and destroy all their metal images and demolish all their high places" (Numbers 33:51b-52).

What is God's chief concern? What is His number one task for them? What will threaten His relationship with them if they don't get rid of it?

Like the Israelites, we live in great proximity to countless idols, most significantly the gods of modern American culture. The life of a Christian must pursue God and God alone, as Jesus emphasized in Mark 12: "'Hear, O Israel: The Lord our God, the Lord is one. And you shall love the Lord your God with all your heart and with all your soul and with all your mind and with all your strength'" (vs.29b-30).

That doesn't leave room for much else, does it?

True worship of God is a lifestyle of turning toward Him and away from the gods of this world. Only then are we acquitted of idolatrous charges. Only then are we truly making sacrificial offerings to God, our Creator, and not the false gods of this world.

✦ LESSON 2 ✦

Take Inventory

"Take a census of all the congregation of the people of Israel, by clans, by fathers' houses, according to the number of names, every male, head by head."

(Numbers 1:2)

Before you begin this lesson, answer the following questions.

Have you ever researched your family genealogy? To what extent?

_____

_____

Do you come from a small or a large family? How has that helped shape you as a woman?

_____

_____

Who are the healthy men over the age of 20 in your family?

_____

_____

Think about the concept of the military draft. Do you know a man who was drafted into service? If so, what was that like for the man involved? If not, how would you feel if one of your close family members were drafted to serve in war times?

_____

_____

Chapter 2: *Take Inventory*

Part 1
Numbers 1

The first chapter of Numbers is often the last chapter of Numbers for many well-intentioned Bible readers. It probably isn't a stretch to say that a phone book is more thought-provoking than this dry census record of the population of ancient Israel (post-exodus, pre-desert wandering).

I confess that the perfectionist, order-loving side of me is fascinated with the neat, categorized report we see in Numbers 1. I'm not sure I can even name my great-grandparents, and I would be hard-pressed to count all the people to whom I'm related. I'm fascinated with the robust, straight branches of the Israeli family tree, despite the boredom that accompanies the reading of them.

If we hover over our foundational knowledge of God, however, we must admit, at the very least, the divine appointment of this chapter in this book in the Holy Bible. We know God well enough to know that His Word is alive and transformative, with every single word of it playing a powerful role in the love story of the Lord and His Church. Despite its seemingly mundane content, then, the Book of Numbers is a God-ordained voice in this narrative.

With that conviction established, let's grab some caffeine and piece out the opening chapter.

Read Numbers 1. Where is Moses when God gives him the command to take a census?

_____

Approximately how long has it been since the Israelites left Egypt?

_____

Specifically, what type of person is being counted?

_____

_____

How is Aaron supposed to list them?

_____

_____

NUMBERS: Wisdom as You Worship

Approximately how many of these men are represented?

_____

Which tribe is exempt from the census?

_____

Why are they exempt?

_____

_____

Can you imagine how awkward and time-consuming this census was? Possibly hilarious, maybe they even teased each other by calling out random numbers to throw off the count, much like a middle-school jokester would. I wonder if they made tally marks on a stone or a tree branch, so they didn't lose track of how many people they'd already numbered off. Can you imagine how many times they may have had to start over? I giggle just thinking about it! I wonder if their conversation sounded something like this:

ELIZUR: Four hundred forty-eight, four hundred forty-nine, five hundred. That's it. 46,500 for Reuben. *(Shouting.)* Aaron! Did you get that?

AARON: Roger. *(Gives a thumbs up.)* Let's see, I'm still waiting on numbers from Zebulun. *(Picks up bullhorn.)* Eliab? You about done down there?

ELIAB: *(Annoyed.)* Not yet, Aaron! We had to start over twice because *(turns toward the crowd and gets louder)*, apparently, SOME PEOPLE don't know how to simply stand still for a few minutes, now do we? *(Some light groaning and a few chuckles from the crowd in front of him.)*

AARON: *(Rolling his eyes and turning the other way.)* Judah? Numbers?

NAHSHON: *(Holding up one index finger in Aaron's direction as he points out individual people with the other hand.)* 74,599 and 74,600. Whoosh! Is that everyone?

(A servant nods.)

NAHSHON: *(Turning toward Aaron.)* Looks like 74,600 for us, boss!
(Aaron nods, licks his quill, and jots down the number on the cypress bark in his hands. He compares notes with Moses.)

What a sight this must have been! Without the aid of DNA testing or ancestry websites, over one-half million of God's people made account for themselves. Amazing!

Chapter 2: *Take Inventory*

With the Promised Land so close they could nearly taste it, it was time for Israel to gauge the size of their army. After all, the native tribes of Canaan weren't going to just hand over their land with a simple **please** and **thank you**. Counting only able-bodied males of age 20 or more, the Israelite army totaled 603,550—a staggering number if you recall how small Israel was when God made His promise to Abraham. Actually, that's a trick question. The nation of Israel had a grand total of two citizens when God promised Abraham that He would build a nation out of him, and both of those citizens were…**senior** citizens, at that. Certainly well-past childbearing age.

But now?

Look at them! Well over a half million soldiers in their army! These numbers alone demonstrate God's faithfulness in keeping His promises!

Let's now examine the one tribe that was exempt from the census.

Look back at verses 50-53. List some of the duties of the Levites.

_____

_____

Look closely at verse 53. Where are the Levites supposed to set up their camp?

_____

Why are they supposed to be in that spot?

_____

_____

From whose "wrath" do you think the Levitical priests are protecting the Israelites?

_____

Why do you think this protection is necessary?

_____

_____

Remember that the Law of Moses required a mediating priest between God and man. The only way an infinitesimally holy God could live among an incredibly sinful people was if there were some kind of cleansing agent mitigating the vast deficit in man's righteousness. His plan wasn't ideal (it would later become made perfect through the once-and-for-all sacrifice of Jesus on the cross, bringing about the new covenant), but His love was unshakable.

NUMBERS: Wisdom as You Worship

Despite this remarkable concession on God's part, Israel's track record for following God's directions is willy-nilly at best. In fact, I wonder if some of the members of the tribe of Levi secretly wished they'd been born to a different son of Israel. They'd seen enough of God's wrath to know that they'd rather battle a squirrelly Canaanite than to have to stand before God again after another Israelite fail.

All of this to say, Numbers 1:54 is beautiful. Finally, God gives directions, and His people follow them.

Write out Numbers 1:54 in the space below.

_____

_____

Why do you think the people completely obey the census directions?

_____

_____

Do you think they understood why they were being counted?

_____

Part 2
Numbers 2

In addition to counting their able-bodied men, Israel received instructions to arrange camp according to tribe. Not surprisingly, God had a specific plan for this, too. No willy-nilly tent staking or haphazard campfires among God's people!

Let's look at God's directions in Numbers 2.

Read Numbers 2. How are the Israelites supposed to organize themselves in the camp?

_____

_____

What are their camps supposed to surround/face?

_____

Chapter 2: *Take Inventory*

Which tribes are to camp to the east of the tent of meeting?

___

Which tribes are to camp to the south of the tent of meeting?

___

Which tribes are to camp to the west of the tent of meeting?

___

Which tribes are to camp to the north of the tent of meeting?

___

Though the precise arrangement of the camps within their cardinal order isn't exactly known, we can get a general sense of the overall shape of Israel's camp from a simple birds' eye sketch.

Dan
(Dan, Asher, & Naphtali)

Ephraim
(Ephraim, Manasseh, & Benjamin)

The Tent of Meeting

Judah
(Judah, Issachar, & Zebulun)

Reuben
(Reuben, Simeon, & Gad)

Look again! Do you see it?

A cursory glance at the camp reveals **a cross**! And what is at the center? **God's presence!** We understand that the tent of meeting was the temporary dwelling place of God's glory, and this most holy space is right at the center of His people. What a beautiful, providential arrangement—a shining foreshadowing of the perfect plan for the **permanent** dwelling place of God and His people, our eternal home in heaven made possible by **the cross**!

Practically speaking, the Levites needed to be spread out among the 12 tribes[1] so that they could, indeed, guard the tabernacle from every angle. After all, entering God's holy presence required protocol, and only the Levites were allowed to perform those rites.

From a spiritual standpoint, however, the integration of the Levites with the warring tribes reminds us of Emmanuel—God is with us.

In us. Among us. Behind us. In front of us. Surrounding us.

Read verse 33. Why do you think the Levites are not among the counted?

_____

_____

Read verse 34. What is Israel's response to God's command for the positioning of the tribes in camp and in movement?

_____

_____

Part 3

Numbers 3

In a moment, we will map where each clan of the Levites was specifically among the tribes, but let's first consider the no-nonsense mentality God had regarding obedience. Though their track record for obeying God was spotty and inconsistent, the Israelites' response to God's positional directions was to their credit.

Probably not coincidentally, on the heels of Numbers 2:34 (about Israel's obedience), we are reminded of a frightening moment of disobedience. As told in Leviticus 10, Nadab and Abihu—two of Aaron's sons—were guilty of giving God something He didn't want. Both Leviticus 10 and Numbers 3 refer to this gift as "unauthorized fire."

What was this **unauthorized fire**? After all, isn't fire...well, **fire**? I have a lot of questions as I consider this. Was it the timing of the fire that was the problem? Or maybe the way it was lit? Or where the fire was offered? Or who it involved?

---

[1] Ephraim and Manasseh were each technically considered half-tribes (as the sons of Joseph), though they are positioned in the camp as full tribes. The tribe of Levi was still one of the 12.

Chapter 2: *Take Inventory*

Details, Lord! I want details!

Maybe I should take a second to explain that the storyteller in me loves the juicy details in any situation. I love a good story, and the more outlandish the details, the better! In fact, if I'm honest, I fight the urge to be a drama queen. (My husband, thankfully, keeps me in check here.) I constantly pray for the Holy Spirit to bridle my tongue and stop up my ears so that I have no part in perpetuating gossip, hurt, or nonsense.

Because—Lord help me—I do **love** a good story.

With that admission, you can understand why I get fidgety with questions over such a front-pager as the zapping of Nadab and Abihu by none other than God Himself. Imagine the talk around camp!

Starved as we are for details, God doesn't leave out the most important point from this story: **He didn't authorize the fire.** We don't know why; we don't know anything else except that the fire was, somehow or another, outside the purview of how God wanted to be worshiped.

The end result? Disobedience. And disobedience leads to one outcome: death.

Read Numbers 3. How many sons does Aaron have? How many can serve as priests? Why can't Nadab and Abihu serve?

_____

_____

Focus on verses 5-10. What responsibilities do the tribe of Levi have?

_____

_____

Whom are the Levites supposed to serve?

_____

What is the responsibility of Aaron and his sons?

_____

_____

Look at verse 15. Who all is to be listed among the Levites?

_____

_____

NUMBERS: Wisdom as You Worship

Indicate in the map below with the positional directions God gives for the location of each son of Levi in the camp. Include:

the Gershonites (verse 23),
the Kohathites (verse 29),
the Merarites (verse 35), and
Moses & Aaron (verse 38).

N / W / E / S (compass)

- **Dan** (Dan, Asher, & Naphtali) — North
- **Ephraim** (Ephraim, Manasseh, & Benjamin) — West
- **Judah** (Judah, Issachar, & Zebulun) — East
- **Reuben** (Reuben, Simeon, & Gad) — South

Around The Tent of Meeting:
- Levites: _____ (north)
- Levites: _____ (west)
- Levites: _____ (east)
- Levites: _____ (south)

What are the specific duties of the Gershonites?

_____

_____

What are the specific duties of the Kohathites?

_____

_____

What are the specific duties of the Merarites?

_____

_____

Chapter 2: *Take Inventory*

What are the specific duties of Moses and Aaron (and their sons)?

_____

_____

Contrast Numbers 1:3 with Numbers 3:15. What is the difference between the census of the warring tribes and the census of the tribe of Levi?

_____

_____

Before God gets into specifics about how each clan of Levi will serve, He clarifies one thing: the dedication of the firstborn. With the original Passover still a vivid memory in their minds, the Israelites were likely anxiously anticipating how God would adjudicate His need for the firstborn of **every living thing**.

"You think Moses will clarify this?" one nervous mother asked a nearby relative.

"Surely. I mean, we've been told not to shed innocent blood, right? My baby is innocent, for sure!" is the quick response. Anxiety is palpable as woman after woman conceives for the first time, only to wonder if God will demand her much-wanted, precious baby once it is born.

If they indeed questioned as such, these women were not far-fetched in their conundrum. God wanted the firstborn and the first fruits of all the Israelites claimed. However, He condemned infanticide, as clearly spelled out in Mosaic law (Leviticus 20:1-5).

So the resolution to this deficit, beautifully, is the dedication of the tribe of Levi (see Numbers 3:11-13) in lieu of child sacrifice. In taking inventory, however, the tribe comes up a few dollars short.

Read verse 39 again. How many males, one month old and older, are among the Levites?

_____

_____

Read verse 43 again. How many firstborn males, one month old and older, are among the warring tribes?

_____

_____

NUMBERS: Wisdom as You Worship

Do the math! How many firstborns is Israel short, in terms of an offering back to God?

___

To make up for this deficit, God requires a redemption price. Read verses 46-48. What was the redemption price per head? How much is collected? What is done with this sum of money?

___

Look again at verses 7, 8, 10, 25, 28, 31, 32, and 36. What word is common to each verse, in terms of describing the chief duty of the Levites?

___

Wisdom for Worship: Taking inventory

God commanded the Israelites to run a census for two groups: the warring tribes and the priestly tribe. He also ordered where they staked their tents, and He delegated specific tasks to the priests. What can we learn from this meticulous process? Here are a few thoughts:

Self-assessment can help us stay ready for the Lord's service, both as an inward evaluation of ourselves and a watchful concern for the Lord's Church. When you look in the mirror, how much of you can be "counted" for the Lord's service?

Think of your schedule, your money, your social calendar, your home, and your talents. Do you see areas of your life in which you are not worshiping and honoring the Lord?

Chapter 2: *Take Inventory*

Consider the Lord's Church at-large. How strong is our army of worshipers? Are our numbers getting stronger, or they falling apart with each generation? What can you do to be sure the Lord's Church is strong in number?

_____

_____

As priests in the Lord's Church (1 Peter 2:9), we have specific tasks. What do New Testament Christians have a responsibility to "guard"? What must we protect and surround and defend? What does this look like?

_____

_____

What tasks need to be done in your congregation? What specific tasks can you do to support, protect, and uphold the work of the Lord where you worship?

_____

_____

If God doesn't want it, don't give it to Him. What does God want from His Church? How does He want us to worship Him?

_____

_____

What are some enhancements that we see some Christ-followers trying to add to their worship? What can we learn from Nadab's and Abihu's unauthorized form of worship?

_____

_____

NUMBERS: Wisdom as You Worship

✤ LESSON 3 ✤

Get to Work

"All those who were listed of the Levites,...everyone who could come to do the service of ministry and the service of bearing burdens in the tent of meeting, those listed were 8,580."

(Numbers 4:46-48)

Before you begin this lesson, answer the following questions.

What is your least favorite household chore? Why do you dislike it so much?

If you work, what is your job? What is the most difficult thing about your job?

Do you minister or work alongside people who do things differently than you do? Does this get on your nerves? Explain.

Are you a rule-follower, or do you go rogue if you see a better way of doing things?

Part 1

Numbers 4

Credited to the famous inventor Thomas Edison is the telling insight that, "We often miss opportunity because it's dressed in overalls and looks like work." I frequently recall this quote when considering my life of worship to God. It's easy to think of holy, God-honoring worship as a blessed time of singing, prayer, and Bible study; certainly, God wants that! But I wonder if I miss beautiful opportunities to worship because they don't exactly look like worship.

Chapter 3: *Get to Work*

In fact, if I'm honest, the more drudgery involved in the task, the less likely I am to think of it as worship to God. Reading Numbers 4 reminds me of the Great Irony—that worship of an utterly holy God often involves the stinky sweat and sticky elbow grease of His creation. Doesn't sound pretty, and it's not the white-robed hallelujah moment that I tend to think of first.

Let's unpack this idea.

Read Numbers 4. Which group of people did this census involve?

_____

_____

In general, what kinds of things were part of "the work in the tent of meeting"?

_____

_____

	Sons of Kohath verses 1-20, especially verse 4	Sons of Gershon verses 21-28, especially verses 24-26	Sons of Merari verses 29-33, especially verses 31 & 32
When the camp is moving, what are they responsible for?			
Census result? (See verses 34-45)			

In theory, I love camping. I love campfires. I love the smell of charcoal grills and wooden matches. I love picnic tables, and I love the soundscape of nature—especially at night: the crackling of the fire embers as they, too, retire for the night, tucked safely inside the fire ring. The soft clapping of the leaves as the trees cheer for yet another stunning performance from daylight. The steady, focused traffic of water through the riverbed and the occasional guffaw from a camper a few sites down who's not yet acknowledged Quiet Hours. I absolutely love it.

In theory.

NUMBERS: Wisdom as You Worship

What I love about camping, actually, is the **rest** of camping—i.e., what happens when the day is over, and it's time to soothe ourselves to rest and relaxation.

Everything else about camping...well, let's just say I try to keep a good attitude while I fantasize about an air-conditioned hotel room and a shopping mall. Dogs barking in the morning before I'm ready to get up—irritating. The heat of the sun bearing down into the tent, roasting me in my sleeping bag—not ignorable. The lone mosquito I managed to dismiss the night before now making his morning smoothie out of my hemoglobin—maddening.

And the bathrooms. Dear heavens, **the bathrooms**.

Apparently, sustainable air circulation is a threat to wildlife because most campgrounds seem committed to keeping it to a minimum in the man-made structures. To reinforce their good stewardship of natural resources, the sink only operates if you have one hand available to depress the spigot with the strength of four men. The toilets are usually standard, but they are meeting houses for mosquitoes who fatten themselves with heat, stench, and moisture.

The showers are probably the most terrifying, however. Usually, there are two options: one small stall with a curtain only half the width of the stall or one disturbingly large stall with a wooden door on angry springs. Showering requires the balance of an adult flamingo because EVERYONE knows that your bare feet must not touch the floor! With visions of ringworm and athlete's foot dancing in your head, you must wriggle out of your shower shoes enough to wash your feet but not enough to touch the brown scum gathering at the one single drain toward which the entire facility slants.

Then you must dry your feet—again, one at a time—while negotiating lunch with the mosquitoes who've been aroused by your fruit-smelling body wash.

So, you see, it's incredibly stressful.

Bottom line: I love the peace and serenity of a still campground at night, but I don't enjoy the inconveniences of camping. Turning even the most mundane tasks into intensive labor, camping is a bold reality check for those who anticipate a relaxing vacation.

I have a feeling the Levites could relate. Worshiping God involved tedious, probably aggravating, and usually disgusting rituals.

Read verse 15 again. What was tricky about the Kohathites' job?

_____

_____

Read verses 46-48 again. How is the work of the Levites described? Copy the phrases that describe what they do.

_____

_____

Chapter 3: *Get to Work*

What worries do you think the Levites may have had in performing their tasks?

_____

_____

What do you think was frustrating, mundane, or stressful about their jobs?

_____

_____

We see elsewhere in Scripture just how serious God was about His directions being followed. Fast forward a few hundred years to the kingship of David over Israel. With his hallmark zeal for Jehovah God, David sent for the ark of the covenant to be brought out among them, after having ignored it during the days of Saul (1 Chronicles 13).

The problem was that a clumsy ox stubbed its toe. Uzzah, one of the cart drivers, reached out to grab the sacred ark so that it didn't fall from the bump, touching the ark with his bare hands. Big mistake! Uzzah's heart seems to have been motivated to protect the holy ark of God—a motive we can hardly criticize.

But when God gives an order, He means for it to be followed. It doesn't matter what your intentions are. God doesn't negotiate His laws, and if following them doesn't seem wise in the moment, we still must follow them over our own ideas.

So, as you may already know or have predicted, punishment ensued immediately. Uzziah dropped dead, and God's message was clear: Unholy hands cannot touch God's holy dwelling place, no matter how well-intentioned we are.

Do you ever find yourself taking shortcuts on tedious tasks? Why or why not?

_____

_____

What kinds of shortcuts do you think might have tempted the Levites?

_____

_____

Based on the story of Uzzah and the ark, do you think God would have accepted shortcuts on this important work?

_____

_____

Read Colossians 3:23. Describe the spiritual aspect of our work ethic.

Part 2
Numbers 5

When I began this manuscript, the entire known world was on alert for a new strand of coronavirus. COVID-19 appeared to spread much more liberally than even the ubiquitous influenza virus.

From a physically neutral perspective, COVID-19 was intriguing in that it seemed to have become a polarizing dynamic in social media, mainstream news, and even the local discount store. On one end of the anxiety continuum were the hyper-vigilant, super-exfoliating handwashers—the ones who stockpiled toilet paper and wore latex gloves to the mailbox.

On the other end of the continuum were the risk-taking, carefree, lollipop-sharing connoisseurs of the chill pill—the ones who reluctantly began washing their hands more often than they shower (to the tune of "Que Sera Sera," of course) and were still trying to organize potlucks at work. They didn't rinse their fruit before eating it because they have the immunity of a well-preserved fossil.

And they were ALWAYS. Trying. To. Shake. Hands. ALWAYS!

Regardless of where we fall on the spectrum of responses to COVID-19, we all can identify with the inconvenience of it. As we are still dealing with it, to be frank, it is a lot of extra work to keep things germ-free! A lot of cleaning. A lot of doing things differently so that this different virus doesn't land in a different place.

Our wonderful God, as it turns out, is a germaphobe.

Completely and utterly holy, He can allow nothing contaminated to enter His presence. Numbers 5 gives us insight into this characteristic of Him, so let's dig in and learn.

Read Numbers 5. What are the three big topics in this chapter?

Why do you think that someone who was unclean physically could not live among God's people?

Chapter 3: *Get to Work*

What work was involved in making things right when one Israelite wronged another?

_____

_____

What major contaminant of marriage did God have a special plan for addressing?

_____

_____

This chapter encapsulates God's vision for peace in our relationships—in our relationships with Him, in our relationships with our neighbors, and in our relationships with our spouses. For peace to exist, however, there must be purity.

Remembering that worship is a lifestyle of devotion to God, that God Himself is utterly holy, and that our proximity to Him is only possible because of His radical plan, we can perhaps understand Numbers 5:1-4. It must have seemed like common sense to any of God's angels who happened to eavesdrop on His dictation of these verses to Moses:

"Seriously, do you really need to tell them that, Lord?" perhaps one angel questioned.

"Shhh. Moses is trying to write," God may have answered.

"But ANYONE with a quail's brain would know not to do THAT!" the angel persisted.

An eyeroll from God and another reminder to **shush** probably sent the angel gossiping to the cherubs about how these people God was adopting must be a few eggs short of a dozen.

But, like us, the Israelites needed things spelled out for them. Coexisting with a holy God was new territory for them, so they needed to be told that you do NOT try to dwell in the camp of Jehovah God if you have a contagious disease or if you have handled a dead body. Take a shower first. Wash your hands. **Clean up before you come to work.**

What are the expectations of your workplace for hygiene and cleanliness? What purpose do these expectations serve?

_____

_____

If you're a stay-at-home mom, retired from full-time work, or you aren't working right now, what are your hygiene expectations and challenges in your home?

_____

_____

What practical purpose do you think God had in mind when He commanded temporary quarantine?

___

___

Part of remaining clean addressed matters of the heart—making things right in relationships with others and with their spouses. This might be the hardest work of all; in fact, in some cases, maybe quarantine is easier than doing the hard work of mending fences with someone you have wronged.

Recently there was a meme floating around social media that went something like this:

> **Things that are hard to say:**
> **I love you.**
> **I'm sorry.**
> **Please forgive me.**
> **Worcestershire sauce.**

I laughed pretty hard at this one, as that last one is the comic relief to the painful reality of the first three. In fact, most of us would probably rather be ordered to say Worcestershire sauce five times with a mouth full of marshmallows than to simply say "I'm sorry" to someone whose feelings we hurt.

Did you catch God's expectation, though? Look at verse 7 again. Not only did God require the Israelites to confess their wrongs to one another, but they had to go above and beyond in their restitution. God's heart seems to be saying, Don't just make things even; make things RIGHT. I hear in this passage a longing in God's heart that His people live among one another in selfless love and intentional forgiveness.

I think it may have been evangelist Billy Graham's wife, Ruth, who, when asked what the definition of a happy marriage was, replied that it's "the union of two good forgivers." That insight resonated deeply with me because it is wrapped in the realistic understanding that flawed people are going to mess up.

Read chapter 5, verse 6 again. When we wrong someone else, who else do we wrong?

___

___

Chapter 3: *Get to Work*

Read Matthew 5:21-24. What does Jesus command with regard to bad blood between two people?

_____

_____

Is there someone with whom you need to make things right? Don't delay! Stop right now, and pray. Pray for forgiveness and for the courage and strength to build peace between you and this person. If you feel comfortable doing so, record your prayer here:

_____

_____

_____

Now pick up your phone, write an email, walk across the hall, or do whatever you need to do to reach out to this person.

The last section of Numbers 5 may be a bit hard to swallow, as it appears to make vast accommodations for a husband's suspicions and jealousy but none for the wife's. Before we unpack the procedural aspect, though, let me offer a slightly different perspective.

Though some may argue that the "adultery test" unfairly targeted women, I see this section of Scripture as God's protection over women. In a patriarchal society, a man owned his wife. We don't quite describe today's marriages in those terms, but the principle of husbands as heads of household is still God's expectation (see Paul's teachings in Ephesians 5). Women today, however, have education and employment opportunities that were lost on ancient Eastern women. Completely dependent on their husbands, these women would be homeless and penniless on their own.

It seems a loving, protective move on God's part, then, to put a system in place whereby a husband couldn't simply feel jealous and punish his wife for adultery that she may or may not have committed. I hear Numbers 5:11-31 as God's way of saying to the men of Israel, **Slow down, Charlie. Before you kick her out, you need to make VERY sure that she is guilty. Your jealousy isn't evidence against her.**

So here is where the laborious process begins. Let's examine it again, keeping in mind God's soft spot for the weak and powerless.

According to verse 14, what happens in a man to justify this process?

_____

_____

According to verse 15, what two things must the man bring to the priest?

___

___

Once she is in the hands of the priest, the following process begins:

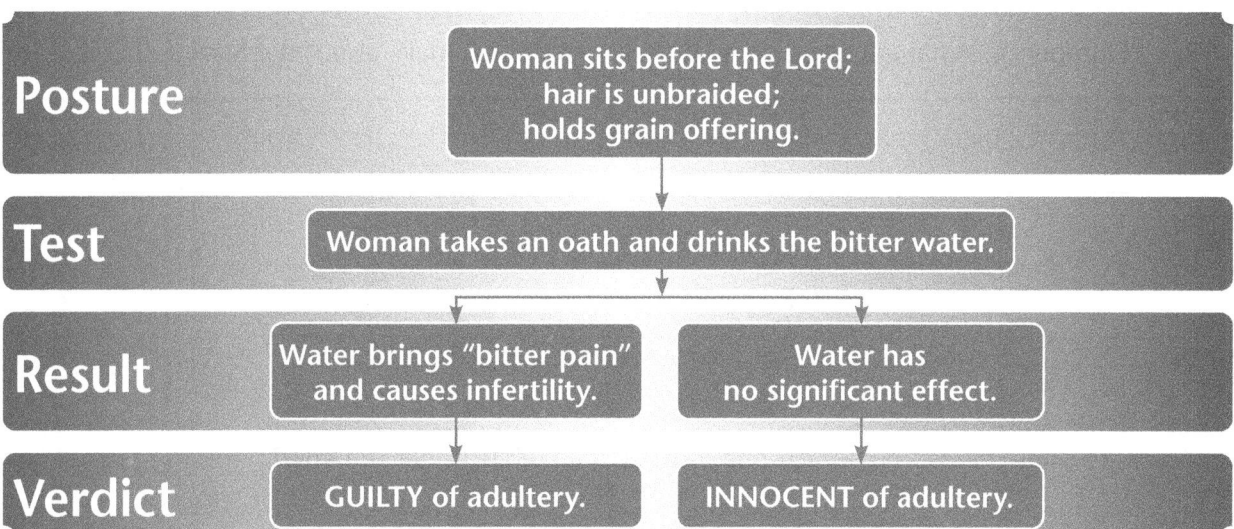

So the process that looks sexist and inhumane to us may actually be a large window into God's high expectations for husbands. There would be no hurtful, willy-nilly accusations of their wives—accusations that could drive the women into destitute lives of poverty and shame. For sincere suspicion, God installed a process. But my guess is that this process deterred quite a bit of unfounded condemnation, to the benefit of many women. Going back to the theme for the chapter, we see God's heart again in that being clean also meant doing right by your wife.

Part 3
Numbers 6

The Nazirite Vow may have been God's suggestion to keep the overachievers in Israel happy, but I'm thinking maybe it was more of an invitation to a season of intimacy with God.

As we know, any relationship takes work from both sides. Let's consider marriage as an example. If you are married, do you and your husband have a way of separating yourselves from others (i.e., the kids) when you have a serious issue to work through? Or maybe it's something relating to others that you need to discuss, but you don't want others to hear. Maybe you need to tackle a financial issue without the distraction of the television or the cell phone.

Chapter 3: *Get to Work*

Whether you are married or single, you can probably recall a time when you needed to discuss something with your boss in private. Some things just need that isolated closeness to address or confidentially protect.

I think of all these examples when I read Numbers 6, where God gives directions for those taking the Nazirite[1] Vow. Let's take a closer look together.

Read Numbers 6. What are some general observations you make about the Nazirite Vow?

_____

_____

Look at verse 2. Who can take a Nazirite Vow?

_____

_____

What are three things from which one must abstain while under the Vow?

(Verses 3-4)   1. _____

(Verse 5)   2. _____

(Verses 6-7)   3. _____

For most people (excluding Samson, whose mother decided before his birth to place him under the Nazirite Vow for his lifetime), was the Vow for an indefinite period, or was it for a specific time of the person's choosing? (Refer to the wording in verses 5, 6, 12, and 13.)

_____

_____

What happened to the timing if one accidentally violated the terms of the Vow? (See verse 12b.)

_____

_____

What must a person do when the Vow is complete? (See verses 13-15.)

_____

_____

---

[1] The term "Nazirite" is not the same as "Nazarene," despite their similar sound in the English language.

Have you ever fasted before? I hope so. I hope you, too, know the power of fasting when you need to work some things out with God behind closed doors, so to speak. Although the Nazirite Vow isn't exactly fasting, we can see several similarities and, thus, learn more about its purpose, challenges, and benefits.

Like the Nazirite Vow, fasting is usually for a specific period of time. My roommate in college used to fast every Thursday, as did others from her congregation. My sister once completed a 40-day fast to work through a significant struggle of hers. Some Christians fast one particular meal each day or on a specific day of their choosing, and some fast for a one-to three-day period. Scripture does not bind us to a specific time frame for fasting, nor are we technically commanded to fast at all.

Interestingly, however, Jesus spoke to His disciples with the assumption that fasting was a regular part of their spiritual lives. Standard translations of Matthew 6:16 and 17 consistently speak presumptively, where Jesus says, "When you fast" in both verses, not "if" you fast. New Testament congregations in Antioch and Galatia fasted for specific purposes, and the Apostle Paul fasted along with them at times and also fasted to grow in his own Christian walk (see Acts 13 and 14, along with Paul's letters to the Corinthians).

Also like the Nazirite Vow, fasting is defined by what it avoids. Most fasting is food-based. Traditionally, a period of fasting means avoiding foods and drinks (except water), though some fast by avoiding certain types of foods (such as sweets). Others fast from food but allow themselves to drink juices, coffee, etc. Some Christians choose to avoid television, social media, or some other distraction as a form of fasting that doesn't involve food. Paul's advice to married couples in 1 Corinthians 7:5 can be interpreted as a type of fast, where a husband and wife agree mutually to abstain from sex for a specific period so that they can devote themselves to prayer.

To our 21st century American culture, the three taboos for the Nazirite may seem a bit random. Why grapes, haircuts, and dead bodies? Why not pecans, scrolls, or one-horned sheep? As we know, God always has His reasons, but perhaps we can appreciate the Vow if we consider the categories represented within it.

- Grapes and wine address the physical demands the body has for food and sustenance.
- Haircuts speak to one's personal appearance and impression to the public; in some cultures, one's haircut tells whether a person is married or single and/or what one's profession is.
- Avoiding dead bodies addresses the cleanliness issue that we've unpacked many times in our study of the Pentateuch: One simply could not approach God without being ceremonially clean.

Chapter 3: *Get to Work*

So regardless of His rationale for the three items, God's invitation provides for a person's abandonment of self-driven, human instincts to abide with Him in holiness for a specific period of time. In the same way that you might go into a meeting at work and close the doors to the outer offices, the Nazirite Vow was a way for Israelites to work with God one-on-one, free from sociocultural demands for the chosen time period.

What types of issues do you think might have prompted an Israelite man or woman to make a Nazirite Vow?

_____

_____

How might a Nazirite Vow affect others—i.e., the family and friends of the person under the Vow?

_____

_____

Have you ever fasted? If so, what was your purpose? If not, why might you decide to fast sometime in the future?

_____

_____

What issues in the world, your family, or your personal life would you like a private meeting with God over, so to speak?

_____

_____

If you were to fast about any of these issues, what type of fast (items to avoid, timing, etc.) would you choose?

_____

_____

Read Jesus' instructions about fasting from the Sermon on the Mount (Matthew 6:16-18). What does Jesus expect when His disciples fast?

_____

_____

I find it interesting that one of the most beautiful blessings in Scripture wraps up the description of the Nazirite Vow. Though you've probably heard it or seen it many times, let's write it out again here:

> "The LORD bless you and keep you;
> the LORD make his face to shine upon you and be gracious to you;
> the LORD lift up his countenance upon you and give you peace."
> (Numbers 6:24-26)

What a beautiful blessing! What more could we ask for than the Lord's keeping, His grace, and His peace? I have these verses underlined in my Bible so that I remember to pray this blessing upon my loved ones.

In the context of the Nazirite Vow, this blessing is especially powerful. If you've ever fasted before, you are keenly aware of the hard thing about fasting: It's hard. Yes, you read that repetition correctly. **The hard thing about fasting is that fasting is hard!** It's hard to deny ourselves, especially of food. Not only do many of our cultural exchanges involve food, but most women—dare I say it—love food for reasons beyond physical hunger. We eat when we're happy; we eat when we're stressed; we eat when we want to, not just when we need to.

I imagine that the Nazirite Vow was equally challenging. With wine and grapes as a staple of ancient Eastern diets, a Nazirite Vow would certainly put a kink in the dinner menu. For reasons that resonate with us even today, denying oneself for the duration of the Vow was hard.

This is why the blessing at the end of the chapter makes me love God even more. It's like God understands the difficult nature of a season of self-denial (whether for the ancient Nazirite Vow or the still-common practice of fasting for spiritual purposes), and He wanted to make sure we were blessed with His protection and His peace whenever we were trying to do so. The beauty of this blessing follows the rigor of the behavior, and we are strengthened and reassured by God Himself as a result.

Wisdom for Worship: Getting to Work

God specified duties for the Levites and gave instructions for staying clean. He even extended an opportunity to dig deep in our relationship to Him, followed by a blessing to us if we choose to do so. How does this inform our worship today? Here are a few take-aways.

Chapter 3: *Get to Work*

Much of our worship looks a whole lot like grunt work. What are some of the things you look around and see Christians doing to help meet the needs of your congregation and God's kingdom at large?

_____

Do you struggle to see menial tasks (like preparing a kids craft or changing the lightbulbs in the building) as worship? Explain.

_____

It takes effort to make things right. How does getting your heart right with God and others impose on your time, energy, and resources?

_____

Do you feel an urgent need to make things right with people as a way of being right with God, or do you tend to separate the two dynamics? Explain.

_____

Deep calls for deep. Does it make sense to you that some of our needs require an extra measure of devotion on our part? Explain your thoughts on this.

_____

What is your biggest challenge in "going deeper" with God? How can Aaron's blessing (Numbers 6:24-26) answer that struggle for you?

_____

NUMBERS: Wisdom as You Worship

❖ LESSON 4 ❖

Make Sacrifices

"And the chiefs offered offerings for the dedication of the altar on the day it was anointed; and the chiefs offered their offering before the altar."
(Numbers 7:10)

Before you begin this lesson, answer the following questions.

In general, do you regularly give your time, money, and talents to your local congregation?

_____

_____

How do you determine what you will give financially?

_____

_____

List several things for which you know your congregation uses monetary contributions.

_____

_____

Part 1
Numbers 7

You've probably already detected the vibe that this lesson will focus on giving. Before you squirm or skip it, however, I encourage you to press through so that you don't miss the incredible blessing associated with giving! But more on that later.

I also hope your eyes will be opened to how much you have to give, even if your bank account shows a negative balance. So many Christians would love to write big checks, but they're struggling to pay the bills and feed their families. **The Lord is compassionate, and there is no limit to His understanding!** (See Exodus 33:19, Psalm 103:8, and Psalm 116:5.) **Do not feel condemned!** (See Romans 8:1.) My prayer is that this lesson will reassure you that no matter your current financial situation, you can worship the Lord through giving.

Chapter 4: *Make Sacrifices*

Worship through giving involves sacrifice. Giving up and going without. Perhaps that means going without an extra car in the driveway so that you can contribute that money to the Church. Maybe that means giving up your Sunday afternoon nap so that you can meet with young people learning to lead in worship. Possibly, it means giving up your pride, your energy, or your guest room.

Let's see what this looked like for the Israelites as God was establishing His presence among them.

Read Numbers 7. In a short phrase or sentence, tell what the tribes of Israel are doing in this chapter.

_____

_____

Look again at verses 2-3. Who brought the offerings?

_____

_____

How many wagon loads did it take to bring the gifts? Refer to verse 3.

_____

_____

If someone showed up to the food pantry at our church building with six loads of canned goods and nonperishable food items, we'd probably say "Wow" and offer a big "thank you!" Even by today's standards, several carloads of gifts for the Church is a big donation. So when we look at ancient Israel's offering to the tabernacle and its work, our jaws should definitely be on the floor.

And they weren't pulling up with beanie-weenies and ramen noodles, either. (Not that those are insignificant gifts!) These were some serious gifts. Gifts that had tremendous dollar signs attached to them. Gifts that required tremendous sacrifice from a humble people. Gifts that probably hurt a little—actually, probably hurt a lot—to give.

There are gifts of money, time, and talent that we give on a regular or semi-regular basis, but these gifts were separate from that. Perhaps your congregation has had a building campaign or another major project, for which they asked for donations above and beyond your normal contributions. I'm thinking the consecration of the tabernacle was that kind of thing, so these offerings were especially sacrificial for the Israelites.

NUMBERS: Wisdom as You Worship

Fill in the blanks in the chart below to form a register of who brought the gifts from each tribe. The first one is complete, as an example.

Verses	Offering Day	Tribal Chief	Tribe
12-17	1st	Nashon	Judah
18-23	2nd		Issachar
24-29		Eliab	
30-35	4th		
36-41			Simeon
42-47	6th	Eliasaph	
48-53		Elishama	
54-59			Manasseh
60-65	9th		
66-71		Ahiezer	
72-77			Asher
78-83	12th		

What do you notice about the gifts brought—did each tribe bring the same gift, or did they bring different gifts?

_____

_____

Using verses 12-17 as a guide, let's break down the gifts:

1 silver_____ (weight=130 shekels)

1 silver_____ (weight=70 shekels)

_____ **offering:** fine flour and oil

1 gold _____ (weight=10 shekels)

Chapter 4: *Make Sacrifices*

Incense

_____ **offering:** 1 bull, 1 ram, 1 lamb

_____ **offering:** 1 goat

_____ **offering:** 2 oxen, 5 rams, 5 goats, 5 lambs

Whoosh! That's a lot of stuff! Multiply that by 12, and you get a lot of silver and gold; plenty of flour, oil, and incense; as well as a grand total of 12 bulls, 72 rams, 72 lambs, 72 goats, and 24 oxen. Animal rights organizations would have had a fit, and it's a wonder the Levites didn't start a petting zoo.

What's the message in all of this? Certainly, God doesn't expect us to dump our fine jewelry and our family pets into the contribution plate each week, does He?

No, He doesn't. The sacrificial blood of Jesus Christ forever eclipsed our sinful humanity, making it possible for us to stand in the presence of a holy God. But the response of giving back to God sets an example for today's Church to follow.

Read 2 Samuel 24:18-25. What was David planning to build for God?

_____

_____

What did Araunah want to do for David?

_____

_____

Why wouldn't David allow this? (See verse 24.)

_____

_____

What does David's response teach us about giving?

_____

_____

Look again at Numbers 7:89. After all the gifts had been brought before the Lord, what did God do?

_____

_____

NUMBERS: Wisdom as You Worship

Part 2
Numbers 8

Sometimes the sacrifices God requires from us cost money. Certainly, in the Old Testament, sacrifices were physical, tangible offerings that had a monetary value attached to them. But if we look closely, we might see that some sacrifices hit a little closer to the heart than the pocketbook. These sacrifices cost us things that are a bit harder to give up than money.

Let's examine this using Numbers 8 as a guide.

Read Numbers 8. In verses 1-4, for what is God giving directions?

Where were the lamps supposed to be set up?

What else did God specify about the lampstand? See verse 4.

Why do you think God specified where the lamps were to be placed?

Why do you think God specified a pattern for the decorative aspect of the lampstand? Was this petty and/or demanding?

What might the Israelite craftsmen have done if God had not given such specific directions?

Chapter 4: *Make Sacrifices*

Before we dismiss this as a persnickety demand from an OCD Creator, let's recall what seems to determine the impact of such a request, at least in Western culture: the degree of intimacy in a relationship between the person making the request and the person who is in a position to grant it. If applying our own cultural understanding to this part of Numbers 8 isn't misleading, I think we will be blessed to see God's tender, protective Father heart instead of a presumptuous, demanding new brother-in-law at Christmas.

Recall that the Israelites didn't exactly have a track record of getting things right, as far as God was concerned. Much like our own human nature, they were "prone to wander" and "prone to leave the God [they] love," as my favorite hymn[1] so beautifully articulates. When they wandered, they tended to wander back to what they knew, and what they knew were the pagan gods of Egypt.

Four hundred years of living among and serving the Egyptians had left its mark. What would have been easy—even without conscious decision making—would have been to create decorations for the tabernacle that looked like the sacred artifacts they'd grown up around. What was sacrificial, however, was giving up their instincts to follow God's game plan.

So I wonder if God specified every square inch of the tabernacle and its decorations as His way of teaching them and protecting them. Teaching them how to craft beauty that didn't flaunt vile images associated with a pagan culture, even protecting them from doing so accidentally. As long as they followed His plan, sacrificing their instincts to honor His ways, they were safe.

To their credit, they obeyed (see Numbers 8:4).

The remainder of the chapter addresses the cleansing of the Levites and the age range for active service in the tabernacle. As I read this, I still hear a theme of self-denial and sacrifice required for God's people to abide in worship. The Levites, for example, had to complete a rigorous cleansing ritual before they could enter the tabernacle. Judging from the extensive process described in verses 5-22, I'm pretty sure they would have also been cleared to also operate on a cardiac patient in the 21st century. They were C-L-E-A-N!

If you or someone in your family is a "clean freak," then you can appreciate the Levitical cleansings. You may remember your mother or grandmother requiring you to take your shoes off at the door, wash up before supper, and be especially clean for church on Sundays. Certainly, as a child, you probably preferred to just run inside, eat dinner, and then run back outside to play—with no time wasted on handwashing and hair-combing. Even though we understand and appreciate cleanliness as adults, to children, habits of cleanliness seem "extra."

In terms of spiritual maturity, the Israelites were still adolescents. The cleansing rituals may have felt "extra" to them, requiring extra time and attention from them. It would have been a whole lot easier for them to do a quick squirt of Germ-X® and then go in to talk to God, and it would surely be a time-saver.

---

[1] "Come Thou Fount of Every Blessing" (Robinson, Robert. "Come thou fount of every blessing." 1758.)

NUMBERS: Wisdom as You Worship

But God would have none of this. Not because He's condescending and controlling, but because He is completely and utterly holy. He can't abide filth any more than a heart surgeon can tolerate the scrub nurses eating a sandwich as they hand over the required tools and clamps during a bypass procedure.

So worship required sacrifice. Not just of bulls and goats and money. But also pride and time and energy. It took a lot of attention to get things right with God, and some of the personal sacrifices may have hit closer to the heart than losing a few pigeons.

Part 3
Numbers 9

Do you tend to speak too quickly? Do you have trouble keeping your thoughts and opinions to yourself sometimes? Do you have the proverbial "foot in mouth" disease?

I sure did. With the patient training of the Holy Spirit, however, the last several years have grown in me a much-needed reflective disposition. Though I still make egregious blunders every now and then, by submitting to the Lord's discipline and by following the examples of a few mature Christian women in my congregation, I have learned to think before I speak. Most of the time, my opinions aren't wanted or necessary. Most of the time, my knee-jerk reaction hasn't yet been bridled by the wisdom of Scripture, so I've learned to hold my tongue and think carefully before I give advice or contribute to a discussion.

Please hear me loudly and clearly: I am still an imperfect work in progress! But I have come to love the Lord's discipline, and I am seeing the fruit of it in this area.

Considering he once murdered a man in a fit of anger, Moses' transformation into godliness is evident in an incident of impressive restraint. Let's look at Numbers 9.

Read Numbers 9. What concern did the unclean men have regarding the Passover celebration?

_____

_____

What does this reveal about the men's desire to obey God?

_____

_____

What is Moses' response (see verse 8)?

_____

_____

Chapter 4: *Make Sacrifices*

What is God's solution to the problem?

_____

_____

I don't know about you, but I am pretty impressed with Moses. Let's not forget how incredibly busy he was. My guess is that he had people coming to his tent around the clock with problems, questions, and concerns. Perhaps some days he felt like a babysitter for a people who faltered regularly in their obedience to God. Maybe on other days, he had writer's cramp from recording God's Law. We know for sure that Moses kept a lengthy docket, wearing himself out in giving advice to everyone who asked for it (see Exodus 18:13-27).

So when some men (who had likely just held a funeral) came to Moses wondering how to still show up for Passover when they didn't have time to go take a shower first, Moses quite possibly was busy and exhausted. He was used to giving advice, so we might expect this question to be a no-brainer for him. He may have been tempted—as I have been so many times—to give a quick answer that fell somewhere within the purview of righteous living.

Yet he didn't.

He told them he needed to ask God and that he'd get back to them. Sacrificing the convenience of a quick answer, Moses punted this one to God. This required more time, effort, and focus than a Google search for Passover laws. I love Moses' heart in all this, though. He wants to get it right, and he will surrender his own schedule to seek God's guidance.

In my role as a high school teacher, I get asked exactly 1,673,492 questions a day—before lunch. The number doubles after lunch. OK, OK, I'm exaggerating, but I do sympathize greatly with Moses in the incessant demand for his guidance, answers, and help. Some questions that my students ask are easy. I can answer them in my sleep because I know my school, my classroom, my subject, and my precious students well enough to spit out a quick reply.

> **Dr. Marvin, can I run back to my last class, please? I left my jacket in there.** (Yes, but make it fast.)
>
> **Do you think 7:00am is too early to start school, Dr. Marvin?** (Maybe, but I love getting out at 2:00pm.)
>
> **Dr. Marvin, what's it called when the story, like, kind of lets you know what's going to happen later on? I forgot.** (Foreshadowing.)
>
> **Dr. Marvin, how many points will I lose if I turn this project in late?** (Same as always. Look at the Late Work Policy that's posted.)

NUMBERS: Wisdom as You Worship

Dr. Marvin, can you tell Bryan to quit being annoying? I'm trying to do my work. (Bryan, quit being annoying and get to work.)

I'm gonna get a tattoo on my birthday, Dr. Marvin. What should I get? (Nothing that you might regret later on!)

Dr. Marvin, Dr. Marvin, Dr. Marvin, Dr. Marvin. (Yes. Hold that thought. No. Be right there.)

They are high schoolers, yes, but their questions are endless. Even as it exhausts me, I love their minds, and I love that they include me in many of their conversations.

There are some questions, however, that I do not or cannot answer without consulting my administrators. Sometimes I know the answer, but it needs to carry the weight of my principal's authority—like for a student whose parent is threatening legal action if her child isn't allowed to turn in a homework assignment that was due a month ago, despite our school-wide late work policy and the two deadline extensions already given to the child.

Sometimes I don't know the answer, so I have to consult my principal before I give a response—like the students who go to New Orleans each year for Mardi Gras and want their absences excused on the grounds of a religious holiday.

I pride myself on my classroom management and my strong rapport with students, so I don't like having to get the "big dogs" involved in anything. Consulting my principals takes extra time—time to type an email or time to go to the office and ask in person. But I have great respect for my administration; they work so hard, and they care deeply about our school. If I need their help, I swallow my pride and push the call button, so to speak.

So I get it, Moses. I feel ya, brother.

Not only was Moses sacrificing his schedule to consult God on this matter, but he also sacrificed his pride. Perhaps these men looked at him with furrowed brows when Moses said he'd have to check with God and get back to them.

"Wait a minute. I thought he was our leader. Why doesn't he know the answers?" one man may have whispered to the other as they headed back to their camp.

"Exactly. Didn't God Himself deliver the Passover law to him? Was he not paying attention? Surely God addressed all of these things. Did Moses really hear Him?" the other one may have replied.

We don't know for sure how the men responded, but I wonder if they doubted Moses at that moment. I wonder if they secretly questioned his credentials, or, conversely, if they assumed he knew the answer already but was putting them off. Or maybe they thought he was being conspicuously pious. These were a people whose short history as a nation included much doubt and fickle loyalties, so it's reasonable to at least wonder if they got a little irritated with Moses here.

Chapter 4: *Make Sacrifices*

But Moses knew who the school principal was, and—busy or not—this was a question above his own pay grade.

Maybe one of the hardest lessons a Christian ever must learn is to WAIT. Sometimes we'd rather God just say NO than to say WAIT. We long to figure life out—maybe then we could be at peace, right? So we ache every day when our longing is met with silence. A line from my favorite movie *Anne of Green Gables* says it well: "The worst would be more endurable than not knowing at all."

Answers, Lord. We want answers. Even if they're bad answers. Just please don't leave us hanging. Please don't make us wait!

How hard is it for you to wait? Are you, by nature, a patient person? Explain.

_____

_____

What kinds of things are hardest for you to wait for?

_____

_____

Is it hard for you to take time in prayer about a complex issue? Is it your tendency to try to fix the problem or talk about the problem before you pray about it? Explain.

_____

_____

Right now a popular trend among women is what I call "the planner movement." Craft stores sell the basic shell—the binder and the calendar pages; then, you have an entire row of stickers, hole punchers, magnets, pens, markers, pockets, and page marks to add to the basic shell and make it personal to you. The result is a beautiful planner, where dentist appointments are softened with a lovely sticker of a tooth, and the annual family vacation is bookmarked with a special "packing list" sticky note. Meetings and ball practices and piano lessons are all beautifully stickered, with times recorded nearby in regal blue sparkle ink. Pulling your planner out of your purse or bag is a proud moment because your to-do list has become the hub for your creative instincts.

Recently I got a hunch that maybe we've gone a little overboard in creating lavish daily planners when I saw a special tote bag designed to carry your planner. But don't we just carry our planners in our purses or work bags? Some even nix the weight all together because they keep their schedule on their smartphone. Why do we need a special bag just for our planners?

Perhaps because we've made a tad bit of an idol out of our schedules? The more we have on our calendar, the more important we feel? And, of course, if I have one of the craft store planners, I tend to schedule more things so that I can use the pretty pens and apply the pretty stickers and have things to put in the pretty pockets.

So when my schedule gets full and beautiful, maybe I do want a separate burden—I mean, bag—to carry. I like the ability to schedule my life and, if I choose, embellish that schedule with my creativity.

I can imagine, then, that some of the Israelites got a little fidgety whenever the cloud covered the tabernacle. Despite its generous shield from the hot desert sun, the Type A women in the camp knew they'd better use pencil instead of pens to mark their personal planners.

Look at verses 17-18. What did the people of Israel do when the cloud was present? What did they do when the cloud lifted?

_____

_____

Look at verses 20-21. How long would the cloud be present over them?

_____

_____

My middle sister and I share a similar tendency toward planning and needing to have dates and times nailed down ahead of time. We would have lost our minds had we lived during this part of God's beautiful story. For people like us, waiting is hard. Uncertainty is harder. And a complete lack of control puts us on medication.

Yet, this part of God's story teaches us. We see in it God's sovereignty and omniscience, keeping His people still when perhaps danger would have awaited them if they had moved and moving them along when their hearts and the world around them were ready.

For the women among them who wanted a predictable pattern of staying or moving, I sympathize. But I am flat out in awe of their obedience in coming and going as the Lord directed, despite the mess it made in their planners.

Wisdom for Worship: Making Sacrifices

God doesn't dwell in a dollar store. We can't buy fellowship with Him with spare change in the car, and His glory doesn't come in a less-costly generic form.

Chapter 4: *Make Sacrifices*

Abiding in worship—living a lifestyle of worship to God—involves making sacrifices. Let's process what this means for today's Christians.

Sometimes the sacrifice is my money. Are you in the habit of making a contribution to your congregation?

_____
_____

How do you feel about the amount and frequency with which you give?

_____
_____

The Apostle Paul tells us to give according to what we have decided in our hearts (2 Corinthians 9:7). Does this freedom encourage or frustrate you? Why?

_____
_____

Sometimes the sacrifice is my will. In what area(s) of your life do you find the biggest struggle between the way you would do something and the way God wants it done?

_____
_____

The new covenant is much less specific than the Mosaic Law. In what ways does this empower the Lord's Church? In what ways can it be dangerous?

_____
_____

Sometimes the sacrifice is my timing. In general, do you struggle to accept God's timing? Explain.

_____
_____

What are things we can do to encourage one another as we wait on God?

_____
_____

✦ LESSON 5 ✦

Stop Complaining

"And the people complained in the hearing of the Lord about their misfortunes, and when the Lord heard it, his anger was kindled, and the fire of the Lord burned among them and consumed some outlying parts of the camp."
(Numbers 11:1)

Before you begin this lesson, answer the following questions.

What kinds of things get on your nerves? What are your pet peeves?

___

___

Do you get impatient or uncomfortable when you're in a large place and among a large group of people? Explain.

___

___

How do you view positive people? Do you tend to judge them and think of them as unrealistic, or do you look up to them for their ability to focus on the good?

___

___

Can you think of a time when the Lord has disciplined you? What was that like? Why was God disciplining you?

___

___

Chapter 5: *Stop Complaining*

Part 1
Numbers 10

There's a Murphy's Law book for teachers somewhere out there, surely. Even if it doesn't actually exist in print, any teacher on the planet can cite most of it by learned experience. And one prominent entry in that book is the Fire Drill Law.

Murphy says that there will always be a fire drill about one minute after you start your students on a test.

The students love it, of course. They get a chance to see the test, freak out, and then go outside and talk about it with their classmates while you, their frustrated teacher, scramble to take roll in a parking lot full of teenagers trying to find their friends that they haven't seen in 14 minutes.

You're outside for longer than usual because admin is trying to figure out which door didn't get closed all the way. Finally, you get the all-clear, head back inside like a group of lazy cattle, and try to get your class to settle down and resume their test (now that they've had the chance to discuss it with one another, thanks to Murphy).

Any teacher reading this knows the other implication of today's fire drill for your class. Now they won't have time to finish it before the bell rings to end this period and move to the next class. Wonderful—said no teacher ever.

It's moments like this that awaken a bit of grumbling from my normally flexible self. I get frustrated and even start complaining that, of all times, this fire drill had to happen during my big, important test.

I wonder if the Israelites were equally well-acquainted with Murphy and his merciless laws. Let's take a look at a couple of scenarios that might have showcased the Hebrew equivalent of Murphy.

Read Numbers 10. What was used as a signaling device for the Israelites?

_____
_____

What are some of the things it was used to indicate?

_____
_____

NUMBERS: Wisdom as You Worship

Look at verse 33 again. What are the Israelites doing here? Where do they end up (see also verse 12)?

_____

_____

How much work do you think was involved in moving the entire camp of Israel to a different wilderness location? Do you think this excited the Israelites?

_____

_____

I kind of wonder if Murphy's Law book for the Israelites included something about the silver trumpet…like, "The trumpet will always blast when you are elbow deep in dough to knead," or, "The trumpet will always signal at the precise moment you've put your wee babes down to rest."

Either way, it seems reasonable to assume that the silver trumpet didn't always rally them at convenient times. It's similarly reasonable to assume, then, that the trumpet blast may have triggered aggravation and complaints here and there. In fact, Scripture offers much evidence that these were a complaining, irritable people.

In Numbers 10, they are about to move again. This wouldn't be so bad, except that they really aren't going anywhere. It's one thing to go on a road trip when there's an exciting destination at the end—such as your favorite theme park or the home of some beloved family members you haven't seen in a while. It's entirely different to drive around aimlessly for several days and end up in an unremarkable place that doesn't look a bit like Grandma's house.

And, bless them, the Israelites weren't just going for a drive. They were moving. What's worse, their forwarding address wasn't yet going to be the Promised Land. Why move, then? I mean, this camp is huge, and it takes A LOT of gas to move it along the desert paths.

Are you serious, Moses? they likely thought and, just as likely, said.

Moses was serious, indeed, because God was. And he was inviting company. He persuades his father-in-law to join them, and then he prays to God for blessings as they travel and blessings when they camp.

Trumpet aside, then, it was time to pack up and set out. And they couldn't just go whenever they were ready. There was a line leader, and they each had to go when their number was called, so to speak. Nothing about this move allowed God's people to sit around idly.

And so off they went.

Chapter 5: *Stop Complaining*

What kinds of irritations do you think the Israelites probably had? What complaints would YOU have had in these moments?

_____

_____

Fill in the chart below to create the line order of the Israelites en route.

[Diagram: REAR GUARD: Dan — [blank boxes] — TABERNACLE — [blank boxes] — FRONT: Judah — 3 days in between — The Ark of the Covenant (God's Presence)]

Do you find any evidence in Numbers 10 that the people knew where they were going or how long it would take to get there? How do you think this impacted their moods?

_____

_____

They say that "misery loves company," which is why optimistic people are annoying to complaining people. How do you think Moses may have been viewed by some of the Israelites?

_____

_____

Part 2
Numbers 11

Every so often the Old Testament gives us a raw glimpse into a surprising dimension of God's character. Sometimes we get so lost in the truth that He is...well, GOD, that we lose sight of His likeness to us.

Or, rather, our likeness to Him.

NUMBERS: Wisdom as You Worship

We are, after all, made in His image. Our instincts, our talents, our appearance—everything about us whispers our genetic connection to our Creator. Naturally, the more time we spend with God, the more we act like Him, talk like Him, and think like Him. But the basic essence of who we are is a dead giveaway as to Whom our Father is.

It should be no surprise, then, that God gets irritated just like we do. Or, to be accurate, we get irritated just like God does. He hates complaining and whining, for example, and so do most of us. Let's take a peek into this part of Him.

Read Numbers 11. What emotion does the people's incessant complaining trigger in God? What emotion does it trigger in Moses? What does this reveal about Moses' closeness with God?

_____

_____

What does God do to the Israeli camp? When does He stop this?

_____

_____

What, specifically, were the people complaining about? Does this sound like the type of thing you or the people in your life would complain about? Explain.

_____

_____

Upon first glance at verses 11-15, Moses may seem like he is complaining right along with the Israelites. Perhaps he is. Perhaps he's missed the curfew God gave him on this pity party, and he's still stuck in a mire of self-absorption.

Another possibility, however, is that Moses was overwhelmed. Burned out. Feeling like a failure. Worried that he had let the Israelites down. Afraid of disappointing the God he loved so dearly.

Have you ever felt this way? Have you ever cried out to God in desperation because you felt like you were collapsing under a heavy load? Do you get afraid sometimes that you aren't able to please God and do what He's called His Church to do?

If I answer honestly, you'll hear an excessively loud YES. And this is where I fall in love with God all over again. His response to Moses is so tender, so full of hope and healing. It is one of many practical examples that shows the truth of Isaiah 40:29-31. God **really does** strengthen the weary. He really does lift up those who are staggering.

Chapter 5: *Stop Complaining*

Two times in Moses' cry to God, he mentions being in favor in God's eyes (verses 11 and 15). What does this reveal about Moses' heart toward God?

_____

_____

What was Moses' specific fear, with respect to the complaints of the people? (See verse 13 and again in verse 22.) How does the Lord reassure Moses?

_____

_____

What practical help does God provide for Moses in this chapter? What does that say about the Lord's compassion?

_____

_____

How does the Lord punish the people for complaining, while at the same time, revealing His power?

_____

_____

Part 3
Numbers 12

The next chapter of Numbers shows us that, as Ecclesiastes says, there is nothing new under the sun. Prejudice, specifically racial prejudice, is as old as humanity itself. This chapter highlights God's staunch posture of anger toward that mindset.

Read Numbers 12. What are Miriam and Aaron complaining about, specifically (see verse 1)?

_____

_____

NUMBERS: Wisdom as You Worship

How does this chapter describe Moses (see verse 3)?

_____

_____

God reminds Miriam and Aaron that He speaks to prophets through, but "not so" with Moses. How does God speak to Moses?

_____

_____

How does God punish Miriam? What impact does this have on the nation of Israel?

_____

_____

Most scholars agree that the ancient region of Cush was in the area we know as Ethiopia today. Many people from that region are considerably darker in skin tone than Middle Easterners. We have evidence from Exodus that Moses' wife feared the Lord; after all, she circumcised her own son to avoid the wrath of God.

Her devotion to the Lord, then, doesn't appear to be the problem for Aaron and Miriam. They seem to be irritated that Moses married a woman from another region, one whose people quite possibly had much darker skin than the Israelites had. What a shallow complaint!

This complaint highlights an ugly instinct we have to criticize or complain about people who are different than we are. Unharnessed, this tendency can be harvested as outright prejudice in the form of racism, sexism, classism, or one of many other "isms."

God's anger burned hotly against Miriam and Aaron, though Miriam seems to be the ringleader. Not only have they initiated complaints (seemingly out of the blue?) against God's chosen leader, but they have also allowed racism to fester in their hearts and become a reason to challenge Moses' marriage.

This hits below the belt because Miriam and Aaron are not two random Israelites. They are Moses' siblings! In fact, it's quite possible that Miriam is the protective, watchful big sister who guarded from afar the basket that their mother had used to hide baby Moses in the Nile. It's quite possible that she is the same sister who offered to go get a wet nurse when Pharaoh's daughter compassionately rescued the baby to raise him as her own. If she is, indeed, this sister, the one who brought Moses' own mother to Pharaoh's house to nurse him, then she—of all people—should have had some sort of sense that God's hand was upon this child, right?

Chapter 5: *Stop Complaining*

She didn't get it, apparently. What she did get was an ugly skin disease. Aaron humbly petitions Moses, and Moses graciously petitions God, Who relents in His anger and doesn't make it a permanent case of leprosy. God is steadfast, however, in His resolve that she needs a Time Out, and He commands that she follow proper protocol for one who is unclean.

What prejudices do people in your geographical area tend to have?

_____

_____

How can we guard our hearts so that we see others through the eyes of our loving Father and Creator, and not through prejudiced hearts?

_____

_____

Wisdom for Worship: Not Complaining

I'm pretty sure the complaining gene was the first to taint our bloodstream after the Fall. It feels as natural a response as any other instinct. God is in the business of transformation, however, and learning not to gripe over petty differences and small annoyances makes us more like Jesus and, therefore, more holy.

We have to do what we have to do. How often do you force yourself to do difficult things? Do you practice doing this just to build your own character and stamina? Explain.

_____

_____

Are you a procrastinator, or do you tackle the dreaded tasks on your to-do list first? Do your tendencies in this area translate to your commitment to God in any way? Explain.

_____

_____

God punishes complaining because complaining is sin. Do you have a healthy fear of God's judgment—a fear that keeps you from sinning and triggers fast repentance in you when you realize you have sinned? What kinds of punishments do you think you may have received for past complaining?

_____

_____

What is a Christ-like way to handle a conversation in which another Christian sister is complaining heavily to you?

_____

_____

Racism and other "ism"s are serious crimes. Discuss how the "ism"s are forms of complaining.

_____

_____

Evaluate yourself and consider how much you tolerate this in your own life. What do you need to do to become more like Jesus?

_____

_____

Chapter 5: *Stop Complaining*

LESSON 6

Anticipate Heaven!

"And Joshua the son of Nun and Caleb the son of Jephunneh, who were among those who had spied out the land, tore their clothes and said to all the congregation of the people of Israel, 'The land, which we passed through to spy it out, is an exceedingly good land. If the LORD delights in us, he will bring us into this land and give it to us, a land that flows with milk and honey.'"

(Numbers 14:6-8)

Before you begin this lesson, answer the following questions.

What is most challenging to you about living the Christian life?

_____

_____

Are you motivated by the hope of heaven, or does heaven seem far off and distant? Explain.

_____

_____

How do you picture heaven? What comforts you most about this image?

_____

_____

Part 1
Numbers 13

Have you ever heard one of those stories about people who have died and then been medically resuscitated, who claim to have seen heaven during the minutes they were out? I don't know if these stories are true, but Numbers 13 makes me wonder. I'm not necessarily defending these accounts; I think I'm saying that it wouldn't surprise me if they were true.

Chapter 6: *Anticipate Heaven*

After all, He let the Israelites unwrap a corner of their Christmas present to see what was inside, so to speak. This vision was intended not only for offensive military preparation, but also for a future hope. Though he wasn't naïve enough to think the Canaanites would leave their turf turnkey, Moses seemed to know already that this land would be abundant in resources—that it would bear much fruit to sustain them (See Numbers 13:20).

Let's take a look at God's sneak peak of the Promised Land!

Read Numbers 13. Whose idea was it to spy out the land of Canaan?

_____
_____

What did God say His intention was, regarding this land?

_____
_____

What kinds of things did Moses ask the spies to pay attention to about this land? (See verses 18-20.)

_____
_____

What was the spies' report? (See verses 27-28 and 31-33.)

_____
_____

What was Caleb's argument?

_____
_____

I tend to be an optimistic person—a highly stubborn one, I might add. If I want something, I make it happen. Where there's a will, there's a way, so to speak, and instead of wishing for certain things, I've always worked for them, as they say.

Don't be impressed! There are a host of problems that come with my disposition, as you well know if you, too, are like this. I can be impulsive instead of cautious. I can be selfish instead of considerate. I can be Martha, the busy bee, when I should be Mary, the abiding companion. Probably the greatest devastation comes when I plow ahead instead of waiting on the Lord.

As a credit to my parents, who never once tried to tame my dreams, even when neither my mom nor my dad had a college education until late into their adult years, my general belief is that **it can be done**. Regardless of what "it" is, "it" can be done. Naturally, then, I have extremely low tolerance for "negative Nelly" and all her friends.

I think maybe Caleb also knew the bittersweet challenge of being fiercely determined and simultaneously annoyed with those who aren't. Of the 12 spies, only Caleb and Joshua had any hope for the Promised Land. Their 40-day reconnaissance resulted in a dismal vote:

> **Who says we go back to Egypt?** (*10 sheepish hands rise.*)
> **Who says try to seize Canaan?** (*Joshua and Caleb raise their hands.*)
> **All right, the vote is 10-2 in favor of returning to Egypt.**

What was so off-putting about Canaan anyway? Wasn't it "the land flowing with milk and honey"? Indeed. Abundant natural resources, however, seemed irrelevant since the Israelites would likely be dead before they could access them. Strong, fortified cities and strapping, robust, healthy citizens—lots of them. No way could the tiny, nomadic nation of Israel take them on! That would be akin to a local quilting guild initiating combat against the United States Marine Corps. A kamikaze mission!

Or so 10 of them thought.

But why would God want to show them the land ahead of time if the consensus was that it was formidable? Isn't ignorance bliss?

My husband and I, along with my two sons, form what mainstream culture calls a "blended family." On our best days, we are fulfilled and happy. On our worst days, we stare at one another agape, wondering what in the world we were thinking when we got married. After all, marriage and parenting are HARD. Turn the heat notch up about 10 times, and you get the even-harder nature of step-parenting and second-marriaging. Though a few wise church leaders gave us a heads up about what types of challenges we could expect to face, we still get the wind knocked out of us EVERY SINGLE TIME one of those challenges rears its ugly head.

In some ways, I'm grateful that we didn't know just how difficult—actually, impossible—some of our days would be. Perhaps it would have filled us with a sense of dread or even discouraged us from marrying each other in the first place.

In this sense, ignorance truly was bliss. We were pleasantly blinded by our love for each other and saw keenly what good could come from our marriage.

Chapter 6: *Anticipate Heaven*

In another sense, though, I'm grateful for the caution we received. We knew to strengthen our spiritual arsenal and put safeguards in place for the hard stuff. We knew the fire would be hot, so we made a steady practice of talking about difficult things.

Sometimes I look at Numbers 13 and wonder why God would dangle the Promised Land in front of the Israelites, only to entice a couple of them but freak out the rest. Maybe His reason was two-fold.

To give them hope.

Let's be real here. The days and nights wandering in circles in the desert were getting O-L-D. *What cruel twisted plan of God's is this?* some of them surely wondered. In fact, some were so "over it" that they said they'd rather be back in Egyptian slavery. They had lost their vision of God's promise to them, and the monotony of manna was flat out maddening.

Doesn't it make sense, then, that our God—Who is full of love and kindness and compassion—would want to raise their spirits? I can picture God as excited as we parents are when we are setting out our children's Christmas presents on Christmas Eve. *I can't wait to see Jamal's face when he sees his new bike,* or *Make sure the camera is ready when Stephanie comes down the stairs and sees her new playset,* we excitedly muse. Surely God felt the same way as the 12 spies trekked toward Canaan. Maybe the conversation in heaven sounded something like this:

They're almost there! They're almost there! Wait till they see the grapes!
I know. I wish they'd walk faster! This is so exciting!
They're about to round the corner—hurry! Get the camera!

OK, so maybe God wasn't rolling with a wireless camera the day the spies made it to Canaan, but I hope you let yourself sink into His excitement. He wanted to bless His children, and He was about to give them an amazing gift! For all their years in the desert, He wanted to give them HOPE of the land to come.

To help prepare them.

Just because 10 of the 12 spies were negative Nellies doesn't mean that their reports were false. Indeed, Canaan was filled with some pretty strong warriors—giants, even. Canaan was the state championship- winning football team, and the Israelites were the local chess club. They certainly had some mojo, but they were nowhere near the size and strength of the Canaanites. And, in their limited perspective, they saw warriors fed on lush vegetation stacked against a people bored with carbs.

In God's wisdom, He showed them some of what they could expect. They'd need their strength, but, more importantly, they'd need their association with Him. The Canaanites weren't just going to hand over their housekeys, and the Israelites would need the Mighty Warrior of all warriors on their side if they were to be victorious.

Wasn't God already on their side, though? Yes, but remember that His presence with them was conditional. Living and dwelling with the Most High, the most holy God cost them unfaltering obedience to His Laws. They could not take Canaan as their own if they stepped outside the protective wing of God. So maybe this sneak peek of the Promised Land was as much a warning as it was a bit of excitement.

This would not be the time to go rogue. This would not be the time to get wishy-washy about God's commands. This was time to suit up and get ready for battle.

So back to the people who die and then come back and claim to have seen heaven... again, I do not know if these testimonials are true or not. But, for some people, they have been a sweet reminder of the hope that awaits us for staying the course with God.

Part 2
Numbers 14

As Christians, we are strengthened by the beautiful hope of heaven. One day—one **glorious** day—there will be no more disease, no more sadness, no more loss, no more sin. One glorious day, we will walk daily with our Lord in His holy heaven. We will worship Him at His throne, and we will—incredibly—eat at His table. Even the animals in His kingdom will experience this eternal peace: former enemies, such as the ravenous lion and the innocent lamb, will nap together and be none the hungrier.

The beauty of heaven is beyond any seaside mansion home on HGTV, for this beauty is not a façade that hides unswept floors and family arguments. Every square foot of heaven is absorbed with the perfect peace of God.

I hope you think about heaven regularly! I hope you even feel homesick for heaven. Setting our eyes on our eternity in heaven strengthens us for the days we live on this earth. Seasoned, church-attending, Bible-quoting Christians might forget, though, that it is possible to jeopardize our citizenship in God's kingdom. We've grown up hearing Bible stories and serving in the church and doing our best to live Christian lives; our place in heaven seems as secure as the same place in the same pew we sit in each week.

But can we lose this promised eternity? Let's learn from the Israelites as they experienced this devastating reality.

Read Numbers 14. Why were the people grumbling and weeping? (See 13:22—14:3.)

Chapter 6: *Anticipate Heaven*

What idea did they contemplate? (See verse 4.)

_____

_____

How did Caleb and Joshua try to refocus them? What was the people's response? (See verses 6-10.)

_____

_____

What was God's first plan in response to their rebellion? (See verses 11-12.)

_____

_____

After Moses talked God out of this plan, what was God's new punishment? (See verses 29-30.)

_____

_____

If you are a parent, you surely understand God's short fuse when it comes to complaining. We often ask our kids to do simple, quick tasks, such as emptying the dishwasher or feeding the dog. Yet—if your kids are like mine—you have heard countless arguments as to why this is the most irrational, impossible, miserable task that they could ever have to do at this moment. **Are you kidding me? This is so simple! All you have to do is take the trash out, and then you can go back to your video game. You're wasting more time arguing with me about it than it would take you to actually take the trash out!**

And yet.

So there it is. When things seem hard or when we are simply "over it," we complain. We are ready to eat our young when they grumble, but an honest look at ourselves probably forces us to admit that **we do the same thing.**

As we studied in our last lesson, God hates complaining. Philippians 2:14 tells us to do everything without complaining. James 5:9 tells us not to complain about one another, and 1 Peter 4:9 challenges us to take care of each other without grumbling.

Are we getting the picture? OK, so back to the nation of Israel.

Despite the fact that they had the most blessed assurance imaginable in the form of God's concrete promise to give them a land of their own, the Israelites started balking.

NUMBERS: Wisdom as You Worship

> It will be too hard. Didn't you hear what they said? The people there are huge! Those people will eat us alive!
>
> Yeah, and then they'll spit us back out because all we'll taste like is this MANNA that I'm totally sick of eating!
>
> Copy that! We'll look like fools marching in there! I can already hear them laughing at us and making fun.
>
> I never thought I'd be saying this, but I wish…
>
> …yeah, me, too…
>
> Well, I'll say it. I MISS EGYPT! Let's go back!
>
> Moses will never take us. You know how he is about things. Fine. Appoint someone else. Any volunteers?

And on it went. Fortunately for them, Moses was a man of prayer, and he convinced God not to zap them like bugs. But God had certainly had enough of all this nonsense. He knew the exact number of hairs on their heads, for goodness' sake; He had provided for them, protected them, guided them, and even abided with them. Yet they still raised their fists and denied the power of God to accomplish what He said He would do.

Worse, they said they'd rather go back. They had a glimpse of the shiny new CORVETTE and said they'd rather drive the lemon.

They had to be punished. You know the story from here. God decides that no members of this original group (those who were a part of the miraculous exodus from Egypt) will ever see the Promised Land, except the two who believed in the power of God, Joshua and Caleb.

What are common struggles that today's Christian women face—struggles that could jeopardize their entry into heaven if they did not rest in the power of God?

_____

_____

What is it about struggle and bondage that makes us return to it sometimes?

_____

_____

What does it mean to "count the cost" (Luke 14:28) of following Jesus?

_____

_____

Chapter 6: *Anticipate Heaven*

What are common triggers for new Christians to backslide, so to speak? How can the Church prepare them for this?

_____

_____

I can't help but shake in my socks when I layer this story on to God's promises for His Church. There is, indeed, a Promised Land awaiting us. A beautiful land! But we won't get to see it if we do not obey God here on earth. If we do not "trust and obey," as the song goes, we will not get to enter our Promised Land.

Part 3
Numbers 15

Imagine that you check your mail one day and are thrilled to find a personal invitation to your favorite celebrity's home Christmas party. Wow! Immediately, after verifying that the invitation is legitimate, you begin planning your outfit, your hairstyle, and even the shade of nail polish you'd like to wear. You feel incredibly honored to be among this star's most cherished fans, and you can't wait to get to know him or her more personally.

Imagine, then, that when you arrive at the party, there are dozens of people there who look…well, who look like maybe they can't even afford a television, let alone party clothes for a bash at a Hollywood mansion. In fact, there are dozens of people at the party who are eating ravenously and even taking turns using the showers. You soon discover that these party guests are homeless, and your admired celebrity is a gracious host to everyone who accepted the open invitation to this year's Christmas party.

Now self-conscious about being overdressed, you are equally embarrassed at having assumed your invitation was just for you and a small circle of others. But your chagrin is short-lived because the celebrity host is making his/her way over to you with a huge smile. Calling you by name—even pronouncing your name correctly—your host eagerly shakes your hand, thanks you for coming, and hands you a glass of eggnog. You can tell by the relaxed, comfortable atmosphere that all guests have been this warmly welcomed.

I wonder if the Israelites were a little bit like a girl in a cocktail dress at a Hollywood party doubling as a soup kitchen. God had painstakingly issued civil and spiritual laws for them, reminding them that they would be blessed for obeying. Imagine their curiosity—perhaps even irritation—when they discover that God intends to offer His blessing to everyone…not just a select few.

Let's examine Numbers 15 for a closer study.

NUMBERS: Wisdom as You Worship

Read Numbers 15. In general, what did God expect His people to bring along with any sacrificial offering? What do you think the purpose of this was? (See verses 1-11.)

_____

_____

These rules certainly applied to whom, according to verse 13?

_____

_____

Surprisingly, to whom else did these rules apply? (See verse 14.)

_____

_____

In fact, in God's eyes, what was the relationship between the Israelites and any outsiders? (See verses 15 and 16.)

_____

_____

I wonder if this was a hard pill for the Israelites to swallow. They were God's people, for goodness' sake. Yet here was God, saying that itinerant strangers were equal in His eyes? What gives?!

Maybe it didn't bother them at all, but at the very least, God's laws imposed on passersby spoke of two things:

First, His heart beat for all of mankind, not just them.

Second, but perhaps a little less obvious to the Jews at that time, was the subtle hint of heaven in that God would be offering salvation to all mankind, not just those of Jewish heritage. His rules for holy living and His path to salvation would be the same for all who accepted the invitation. Regardless of social status or cultural upbringing, every single one of us has a seat at God's grand buffet should we choose to accept His invitation.

As we keep our hearts and our minds on heaven, let's remember a few things: We must stay in fellowship with God and keep food on His table, there are rules on how we get there, and we won't get there if we don't follow them.

Chapter 6: *Anticipate Heaven*

Do you enjoy being singled out as special, or do you prefer to share attention with a like-minded group? Do you prefer a clear-cut winner, or are you OK with a tie?

_____
_____

In what way do people in our culture feel territorial about the rights of citizenship? Do Christians feel this way at times?

_____
_____

How does a competitive spirit hinder our vision of heaven?

_____
_____

Wisdom for Worship: Anticipating Heaven

God's Word gives us glimpses into the construction going on in heaven, but beyond descriptions of the physical space, God consistently tells us the greatest benefit of our Promised Land: eternity in His presence. This promise, however, isn't unconditional. Living and dwelling with the Most High, the most holy God costs us, too. Like the Israelites, we must embrace God's laws and walk in obedience to them. The difference for us is that the sacrificial blood of Jesus Christ means that our laws are less cumbersome. Jesus' death was the Sacrifice to end all sacrifices, the Blood to replace all bloods. Covered by His payment, we are welcomed in the presence of God if we, too, turn from sin, put on Jesus Christ, and embrace worshipful, Christian living.

I credit the wise pulpit minister at my congregation, Tim Alsup, with the insight for our first take-away from this section of Numbers.

God's love for us is unconditional; His salvation is not. It requires obedience. Do you get afraid, annoyed, or overwhelmed by the cost of discipleship to Jesus Christ?

_____
_____

NUMBERS: Wisdom as You Worship

Do we take for granted our citizenship in heaven, forgetting the tremendous cost involved?

Complaining threatens our joy and hope. Do you complain about things in your Christian commitment? (A sermon you didn't like? A song leader who was off-key? A potluck that got canceled?) How does this affect your joy in the Church?

How do we sometimes justify complaining? In doing so, are we sinning? What does deliberate sin do to us?

The land is beautiful! Get excited! How can you nurture your excitement about heaven? How can you share this enthusiasm with others?

Are you easily overwhelmed by the hardships in this life? How can the hope of heaven invigorate your soul?

There are Calebs and Joshuas in the Church—listen to them. Who in your life consistently keeps a God-centered focus? What does this look like?

Chapter 6: *Anticipate Heaven*

Why is it easy to get sucked into negativity? What is one thing you can do this week to turn your ear more toward a Caleb or a Joshua in your life?

_____

_____

LESSON 7

Watch Out

"...You have gone too far, sons of Levi!"
(Numbers 16:7)

Before you begin this lesson, answer the following questions.

Is jealousy a struggle for you? Why or why not?

_____
_____

Do you have trouble respecting authority in certain situations? Explain.

_____
_____

In general, do you cower or stand firm when someone challenges your authority?

_____
_____

Part 1

Numbers 16

I remember goofing off with my dad one day when I was a child. He was teasing me, and I was pretending to be appalled. At some point in the harmless back-and-forth, I rolled my eyes, laughed, and said, "Oh, shut up!" in the same lighthearted tone of voice I would use with my best friend.

Chapter 7: *Watch Out*

That abruptly ended our joking because my dad raised his eyebrows, shook his head, and told me sternly that I had gone too far. In no uncertain terms, I learned in that moment that "shut up" was something you never say to your parents—even if you are just kidding around. I learned that there are some lines of authority that you just don't cross.

The Israelites had a similar wake-up call, but, unfortunately, their correction didn't land in the context of harmless joking. Let's see what this looked like as we continue our reading of Numbers.

Read Numbers 16. What were Korah and his men challenging? (See verse 3.)

_____

_____

What was Moses' response?

_____

_____

What was God's reaction to Korah's attitude?

_____

_____

What "test" did Moses arrange so that the people would know that his authority over them came from God?

_____

_____

How did this "test" turn out?

_____

_____

Did the Israelites' attitude change after Korah's destruction? (See verse 41.)

_____

_____

NUMBERS: Wisdom as You Worship

This chapter captures what might be my favorite Moses-moment in all of Scripture. I am so impressed by his humility and his persistent posture of **turning toward** the Lord. In the face of in-your-face criticism, I'm sure Moses had to swallow his own insecurity to uphold God's plan. Perhaps the conversation went something like this:

> **Korah:** "What makes you so special? If what you say is true, we are ALL God's people. Who do you think you are, Mr. I-Killed-a-Man-One-Day? Why should we listen to you, especially when all we're doing is wandering around this blasted desert!"
>
> **God:** (*softly to Moses, who is shaking inside*) "Forget who you were and remember who you are, Moses. Speak boldly."
>
> **Moses:** "Let's let God show us Himself the person He has picked to lead."

And so on. Non-stop complaining has morphed into outright rebellion, and God is about to show them what's what. He causes an earthquake to swallow up the ringleaders, sends fire to consume the hotshots, and spreads a plague to destroy a good many complainers. Only the prayerful, humble, gracious intervention of Moses and Aaron—the current priesthood, whether the Levites liked it or not—keeps God from annihilating the jealous wannabes of Korah.

We have the advantage of the entire book of Mosaic Law—and all of Scripture, for that matter—when we react to this scene with horror. *Are you nuts?* I think every time I read this chapter. *Don't you know ANYTHING about the God Who keeps you? You'd better watch out!!!*

But my aerial view of this brazen spiritual recklessness is heavily padded with the Big Picture of Scripture; additionally—and conveniently—I am far removed from this conundrum. The sons of Korah, on the other hand, were immersed in it and had not even entered Canaan yet, much less contemplated God's master plan for salvation for all.

I can sympathize with them even more when I realize how very much like them we are. Let's use an example that is a pressing topic in many churches today: women in church leadership.

First Corinthians 14:34-35 and 1 Timothy 2:8-14 indicate that God's plan for leadership in Christ's Church is to be fulfilled by men. Women, and sometimes even men, often challenge this plan with statements like the following:

> **Why can't a woman lead singing when plenty of them sing better than the men who lead?**
>
> **What's the harm in an organized, business-savvy woman being a deacon? Women are just as capable as men! This is sexist!**
>
> **Women have just as much ability to interpret Scripture as men. Why can't they preach?**

Chapter 7: *Watch Out*

Ladies, whether you've ever wrestled with this or not, let's agree on a common tendency for many women, in general: If someone isn't doing it right or how we like it done, we'd rather do it ourselves.

Our children can attest to this, as they quickly learn how to do a sloppy job on a chore so that they lose the "privilege" of folding the towels or whatever. I'll fess up to a parenting fail of my own: getting my kids to clean their rooms. Actually, when I told them to clean them, they did so; however, their standards were significantly different than mine. I had in mind a gut job, Marie Kondo-style. Their satisfaction, however, was easily obtained by clearing a path to their bed and taking a few dirty dishes to the kitchen sink.

Eventually, both my boys would slyly ask me to clean their rooms for them. And—again, probably a major fail on my part—when they'd go visit family each summer, I'd slither into their rooms and clean them **my way.**

Here's the worse part, as far as our analogy to church leadership is concerned. My way of cleaning their rooms was indeed better, and my boys came to love it. They would come home from their trips and just lie on their beds or sit on their lounge chairs for a bit, taking in the peace and order of their personal space. Mom had cleaned, organized, labeled, and purged every nook and cranny of their room, as if staging it for a magazine photo shoot.

So why was that so bad? Because I did it for them. Because it really was their job. Because when I did it better, we all became convinced that only Mom could clean a room correctly.

Because God has gifted women with a pretty strong mojo to take charge when necessary, I think our congregations could fail similarly if we dipped our toes in the waters of church leadership. God never said women aren't capable of leadership, teaching, and spiritual insight. Indeed, we could probably do a pretty good job—maybe even better than this man or that man.

Why would this be a problem? Because it's not our job. God's plan is to teach men how to clean their own rooms, so to speak, not have their mamas do it for them. It is the job of men to lead, even if a more qualified or talented woman is nearby.

So even though it's easy for me to look down on Korah and scream warnings to them about challenging God, I need to step back and consider areas of God's plan and my life about which I perhaps routinely challenge God. The root of Korah's rebellion and the root of my own are the same, and both hold the dangerous potential to incite the wrath of our sovereign God.

"I am Who I am," God explained in Exodus 3:14. And that settles it.

Are there areas of church worship or leadership where you question Scripture's directives? What are those?

_____

_____

In what areas of your life do you struggle to trust God?

_____

_____

Do you get irritated by the leadership at your workplace? In your congregation? In your family? What is a Christ-like mindset to take in these situations?

_____

_____

Part 2
Numbers 17

Imagine this: You leave your children home alone for a couple of hours while you run some errands. Prior to leaving, you tell your middle child, who often complains about being bossed around by her older sister, that she will oversee keeping up with the list of chores you've left on the counter. You've put the children's names on the list, assigning each child three chores to complete by the time you get home.

All your middle child has to do is be "the checker." She gets to check the chores off the list as your children complete them. Though she takes pride in the role, it literally involves no authority. She's just taking a pencil and putting a checkmark beside each chore as it is done.

You've barely made it out of the driveway when your phone rings. It's your dear middle child, mad as a hornet because her older sister and younger sister are challenging her right to be the checker of the list. You hear screaming in the background, and you order your middle child to put you on speakerphone so you can lay down the law for everyone.

"**She's not the boss of me!**" your oldest exclaims.

"**She keeps calling me a baby! She says I have to do her chores, too, if mine aren't done right!**" your youngest insists.

"**Did not!**" your middle child hisses, and by now all three of three of them are fighting like cats.

Chapter 7: *Watch Out*

As you wave to your neighbor, who's breezily jogging on the sidewalk despite the sub-freezing temperatures outside, you manage to call your kids to order and bark out the terms for a truce:

"Everyone pick a number from 1-10, but don't yell it out," you say, glancing at your rearview mirror as your neighbor's long, beautiful, perfect ponytail sashays back and forth behind her. You can feel a migraine coming on.

You pick the number 4, rationalizing in your mind that your middle child was born in April, the fourth month.

Oldest child calls out the number 7. Middle child, incredibly, calls out 4. Youngest child complains that she wanted 4, but you tell her to hush and pick another number. She picks 9.

Middle child wins. Her authority and her pencil are restored, and you threaten them within an inch of their lives if they don't settle down and get their work done.

Right before you hang up, you hear your oldest child mutter, **"You love her more than us."**

Your head is throbbing by now, and you pull into the grocery store parking lot, completely forgetting what you needed to buy.

If this scenario resonates with you, you can appreciate the headache Moses had when the people of Israel challenged his and Aaron's authority as leaders.

Read Numbers 17. What did God collect from each of the 12 tribes? What were the tribal chiefs supposed to write on them?

_____

_____

What did God intend to show Israel, using these staffs? What would happen to the staff of the leader He chose?

_____

_____

Whom did God prove to be the priest He chose?

_____

_____

NUMBERS: Wisdom as You Worship

What did the Israelites mutter after this whole ordeal? (See verses 12-13.)

_____

_____

One thing we need to guard in our hearts is our willingness to submit to authority. In the case of Numbers 17, the Israelites were struggling to with a who-does-he-think-he-is attitude toward both Moses and Aaron. They didn't like their current situation and challenged the credentials of their leaders, as a result.

As you can tell from the passage, this doesn't go over well with God. In fact, He's irate at the audacity of His people to question Him at this point in their miraculous journey. For the sake of Moses' and Aaron's sanity, however, He gives a visible sign to, hopefully, squelch for good the complaints over who's in charge.

Not surprisingly, the people's response is, essentially, **"You like Aaron more than us."** Good grief!

You might be able to sympathize with the Israelites, and you totally get God's irritation. Ironically, there's something in us that doesn't like our own authority being challenged, yet we are not far removed from the instinct to question someone else's.

This is where we need to be very, very careful. Let's take a minute and reflect on the center of a woman's world—her home.

Read 1 Corinthians 11:3 and Ephesians 5:23. Whom does God appoint as the leader in our marriage and in our home?

_____

_____

Why is letting the man lead in our homes hard sometimes—maybe hard **often**?

_____

_____

What tasks or responsibilities do you think belong exclusively to a husband, in keeping with God's plan for him as head of the household?

_____

_____

Chapter 7: *Watch Out*

Whom are we really challenging or rebelling against when we don't submit to our husband's authority?

_____
_____

What can you do this week to encourage your own husband in his God-appointed role? If you are single, which married woman can you pray for this week, upholding her as she tries to love her husband?

_____
_____

Part 3
Numbers 18

At some point in our lives, we've all been warned to "be careful what you wish for," haven't we? My first thought when beginning Numbers 18 is this ages-old maxim. After all, why would anyone want the tremendous responsibility that Aaron and the Levites bore? As the Israelites complained and whined and insulted and sassed, did they have any idea what Aaron and Moses were actually doing on their behalf?

Something tells me that if they really understood the weight of the priesthood, they'd back off like frightened cats. Who, of any of us, would sign up to literally bear the sins of God's people? And which one of us in our right minds would have fought for the right to guard the presence of God Himself? What a terrifying responsibility!

Now that God has given the people an unmistakable sign that Aaron is His appointed high priest and the Levites are the collective priesthood, let's take a look at their job description...I have a feeling no Israelite would wish for it.

Read Numbers 18. What are the two chief responsibilities of the Levites? (See verse 1 and verses 4-5, also verse 23.)

_____
_____

NUMBERS: Wisdom as You Worship

What job did God give Aaron, specifically? (See verse 8.)

_____

_____

What would the Levites NOT receive from the Lord? How would their needs be met? (See verse 20.)

_____

_____

If the Israelites had any idea just how much of a favor Aaron and his brood were doing for them, they would have started a list on TakeThemaMeal.com, volunteered to babysit their kids, and taken turns cleaning their tents. In other words, they surely would have gone out of their way to show their gratitude and make things easy for the Levites.

To grasp this awesome, humbling role, let's use a visual.

Chapter 7: *Watch Out*

Remember from our study of Leviticus (*Leviticus: Directions as You Decide*)[1] that God did not issue forth a multi-volume legal code just because He's nitpicky. Though some people today mistake God's sometimes-seeming interminable laws as "just a bunch of dos and don'ts," a close look shows the tremendous miracle these laws represent.

God—utterly and perfectly holy—longed to dwell among His creation, which was working out all fine and dandy until Adam and Eve disobeyed God, bringing sin into the heart of man.

A pristinely righteous God can no more co-mingle with sinful people than oil can mix with water. It just can't work.

But God is stubborn. And so is His love.

To recap, this is where Leviticus comes in. All the laws for sacrifice and holy living were GOD'S LOVING PROVISION for His people so that He could dwell among them. It wasn't a perfect solution to the disunion of holiness and sin, which is why God would eventually send His Son Jesus to be a once-and-for-all sacrifice that would give us all rights to enter His holy presence and be called His own.

But I'm getting ahead of myself. Back to the visual!

In God's makeshift sanctuary, there HAD TO BE mediation between man and God. The High Priest would carry the sins of the people before the presence of God—a terrifying responsibility! The remaining priesthood would protect the High Priest and the parameters of God's presence. They would stand—actually, live and work and serve and labor—in the vast gap between God and man.

Whoosh.

Think of a leader in your life. Maybe your husband, as the head of your household. Maybe your boss, as the authority in your workplace. Maybe an elder in your congregation or an official in your community. Try to imagine yourself in this person's shoes. Write out all the things this person probably worries about on a given day.

Now process what that leader does for you, whether directly or indirectly. List what comes to mind.

_____

_____

Do you think this leader ever feels underappreciated and taken for granted? Why or why not?

_____

_____

[1](Marvin, 2019)

Challenge: Think of something you can do this week to encourage this leader.

Wisdom for Worship: Watching Out

Leadership comes with enormous responsibility. Many of us would be aghast if we truly understood the weight that God's appointed leaders carry! We may challenge their authority, nag them, or dismiss them; we may go so far as to "do it ourselves" because we're impatient and offended. God's plan for leadership in His Church and in our homes is established, however; it is not up for negotiation, no matter how much better we think we could do on this job or in that role.

Not accepting God's plan is ugly pride on a date with rebellion. We try to justify our motives or explain our intentions, but God calls it SIN. And how can we draw near to our most holy God with sin in our hearts?

God has given us leaders in the church and in the home. We must trust those leaders. What about the elephant in the room—i.e., the husband who isn't a Christian or the preacher whose lessons are dry as dust? What then?

What does respecting and submitting to male leadership look like, in a practical sense, in the church? In the home?

_____

_____

We are in rebellion against God if we do not trust His sovereignty. Do you think God gets angry at our rebellion like He did the sons of Korah? If so, how would He punish us?

_____

_____

How should we respond to arguments and bickering against the leaders in our lives?

_____

_____

Chapter 7: *Watch Out*

God's plan is clear. We are prone to misinterpret, misapply, and/or flat-out disobey it. Where are you tempted in this way? Where do you need to "watch out" so that your life of worship to God is not silenced by sin?

_____
_____

Give an example of a scriptural command that we often see twisted or distorted by Christ-followers.

_____
_____

❖ LESSON 8 ❖

Stay Hydrated

"Now there was no water for the congregation.
[A]nd the LORD spoke to Moses, saying,
'[T]ell the rock before their eyes to yield its water. So you shall bring water out of the rock for them and give drink to the congregation and their cattle."
(Numbers 20:2a, 7, 8b)

Before you begin this lesson, answer the following questions.

Describe your baptism into Christ. If you have not yet been baptized into Christ, discuss what thoughts you have as you contemplate that decision.

_____

_____

Is it a struggle to wait on the Lord when you find yourself in need? Explain.

_____

_____

Is it hard for you to picture the loving, longing heart of God toward you? Explain your general understanding of God and what has influenced that perspective.

_____

_____

Chapter 8: *Stay Hydrated*

Part 1
Numbers 19

The simple truth is that we can't live without water: We can't keep our bodies clean or hydrated. We can't keep the earth's ecosystems balanced, and we can't produce food.

I love the image we get of God in Genesis 1. Before Creation even begins, we see God "hovering over the face of the waters" (Genesis 1:2) like a nervous parent. Pre-dating Creation are two entities: God and water.

We cannot live without either one of them.

Fast forward from Creation to the wanderings of the nation of Israel, post-exodus. As God lays out the rules for purification, He predisposes mankind to the role water will play in the ultimate cleansing of our baptism into Christ.

Read Numbers 19. After making the sacrifice to God for Israel's rebellion, what did the priest Eleazer have to do before he could return to camp?

_____
_____

What did the person who actually burned the animal have to do before reentering camp?

_____
_____

What was the purpose of saving the animal's ashes?

_____
_____

What did the person who gathered these ashes have to do to cleanse himself?

_____
_____

NUMBERS: Wisdom as You Worship

What did the cleansing rituals for touching a dead body or coming near a dead body have in common? (See verses 11-19.)

_____

_____

What was the consequence of not following the cleansing rituals?

_____

_____

You don't have to be around church for long before you realize what is absolutely essential to our right standing with God. Under the new covenant, the blood of Jesus Christ serves as our one-time sacrifice—a perfect, complete offering to forever cover us in the presence of a holy God.

It's not an automatic gift, though. All dogs do NOT go to heaven, as it turns out. Despite how soothing it may be to think about when we lose a loved one or contemplate our own eternity, not everyone goes to heaven. Someone who has lived her life as "a very good person" is no more guaranteed citizenship in heaven than a Sasquatch is.

Our own goodness—as you've hopefully learned—is completely insufficient to bring us in right standing before a holy God. In fact, the prophet Isaiah compared our best behavior to the sweaty, sour, nasty underwear we have during "that" time of the month (Isaiah 64:6).

The blood of Jesus Christ is a free gift, but there's a string attached. There must be, if you think about it, because the whole purpose of it is to connect us with God. If you're bothered by this idea, just picture God at one end of the "string" and you at the other end.

The condition for this gift is that we confess our belief in Jesus Christ, repent of our sins, and be baptized into Christ. This complete process—not just part of it—cleanses us from our sins and places us, incredibly, in right standing with God.

We must guard against ever minimizing the importance of belief and repentance in the process of becoming a Christian. If one is baptized but doesn't believe in Jesus Christ, she is not saved. Belief and repentance are absolutely essential (John 8:24).

That belief and repentance, however, leads us to obey the gospel and subject ourselves to the rite of baptism.

Chapter 8: *Stay Hydrated*

Have you been baptized into Christ? If so, describe what that means to you. If not, what keeps you from taking that step?

_____
_____

What is a common religious explanation about "how to be saved" without necessarily being baptized?

_____
_____

Read 1 Peter 3:21. What defines our salvation experience?

_____
_____

Through what did God bring Noah and his family to save them from damnation? Through what did God bring the Israelites to save them from slavery? (The answer is the same for both!)

_____
_____

Part 2
Numbers 20

Nik Wallenda knows what it's like to be on a perilous journey. In fact, you may have watched him on television crossing Niagra Falls on a high wire or inching across the Grand Canyon on a tight rope no wider than your thumb. To date, he's successfully crossed many famous chasms in this fashion; whether that's a miracle or insanity is a matter for friendly debate.

Granted, Wallenda's "journeys" measure only the length of a country driveway, but if you've watched him for even a minute, you know that those trips take a l-o-n-g time. A three-toed sloth could shower and get dressed twice in the time it takes Wallenda to make it even to the halfway point.

NUMBERS: Wisdom as You Worship

That's part of his success formula, however. Never in a hurry, he paces himself with deep breaths and outspoken praises to God every time he advances his toenail. If the wind causes the rope to sway, he pauses. If he loses his precarious center of gravity, he stops and refocuses.

Amazingly, he makes it across, usually in the span of a couple hours—during which time none of his fans have exhaled—and excitedly sets both feet square on terra firma in victory.

But what if you or I were asked to make such a trek? Maybe you're a yoga guru and can outbalance a flamingo, but I'd be lucky to make it across the length of a bathtub. But what if Nick Wallenda himself assured you or I that we absolutely would make it to the other end of the high wire as long as we kept eye contact with him and followed his directions to the proverbial T?

I don't know about you, but I have a feeling my enthusiasm would last maybe two steps before I realized I was in WAY over my head. As my realization manifests itself as panic, Wallenda tries to reassure me to focus on him. He reminds me that I must follow his directions. In fact, he's walking ahead of me, backwards, so he can keep an eye on my every move.

Despite his Guinness-level of expertise and regardless of the tether that gently rolls behind me, I start fussing and whining and getting outright hysterical. **"Are you trying to kill me?"** I cry.

Sometimes I wonder if the Israelites felt like they were being led across Times Square on a high wire. The desert land was arid and hot, and they were traveling long hours only to arrive at nowhere. God kept assuring them that they would make it to the other end of the rope, so to speak, but that promise of a bountiful land to call their own meant nothing to them when they were thirsty. Let's read Numbers 20 and see how God gets them across this leg of the journey.

Read Numbers 20. What was the Israelites' biggest complaint while at Meribah?

_____

_____

Before answering the people, what do Moses and Aaron do?

_____

_____

Chapter 8: *Stay Hydrated*

What was Moses supposed to do to meet the people's need?

_____
_____

What did Moses actually do?

_____
_____

What was God's punishment for Moses' disobedience?

_____
_____

How does Moses attempt to ease the people's journey? Does this plan work?

_____
_____

I love that the Lord allowed His people to get so thirsty. Granted, thirst would be a given during desert travel, but at Meribah, they were dehydrated and desperate. The parallel need we have for Jesus Christ, our Living Water, is unmistakably foreshadowed in this moment. We wander; we roam; we die of thirst for significance, for fulfillment, for answers, for everything that matters. We are tempted to return to the things that enslaved us in the first place, yet our sustenance and hope comes from a Rock, of all places.

The Rock of Ages, as it turns out.

What do you tend to turn to when you are stressed? Is this helpful or hurtful to your soul?

_____
_____

Why do you think Moses struck the rock instead of just speaking to it, as God had commanded him? Can you identify with this level of stress and frustration?

_____
_____

NUMBERS: Wisdom as You Worship

In what ways are believers still sustained by the water of life, even long after their baptism?

What role does worship play in quenching our spiritual thirst?

Part 3
Numbers 21

The hardest part of the COVID-19 crisis has been the isolation. Never again will I take for granted the healing power of a hug. Never again will I take for granted the strength I feel during corporate worship. Never again will I take for granted the hundreds of kids I am around each day when I'm teaching from my classroom, not from my laptop.

I was caught off guard, then, when our first Sunday back in the pews of our church building made me sad. We were spread out, and our elders had carefully structured every aspect of the service so that we stayed in step with the health department's advice for social distancing. We were about half and half with masks, and when service was over, we all filed out of the auditorium like a graduation recessional.

My sadness, I realized, was that we were together, but we couldn't be together. Masks covered encouraging smiles, and reassuring hugs were off limits. Sweet fellowship and conversations were replaced with waves in the parking lot. That Sunday made me realize just how thirsty I am for the strength of the assembly of the people of God.

Let's look at Numbers 21.

Read Numbers 21. What small victory does God give His people after Aaron's death? (See verses 2-3.)

Chapter 8: *Stay Hydrated*

When the people started complaining again, how did God punish them?

_____

_____

How did God restore them after this time of hardship? What did He want to give them?

_____

_____

What moderate victory did God give the Israelites after they were refreshed at the well?

_____

_____

Many of us are still so thankful for livestreaming Sunday worship and preaching, which became more of a thing during the COVID seasons. Because of this blessing, we were able to study the Bible in step with others in the congregation, despite the quarantine mandates.

Once Amazon and Christian retailers ran out of the portable emblems of the Lord's supper, several of us ladies in our church passed around a recipe for communion bread. Making it on Saturday nights after everyone else went to bed became a quiet, sweet time between God and me.

But the singing, though. That was a struggle.

Most people in my family can stay reasonably on tune, so cacophony wasn't the problem. I'm ashamed to say that we never quite got over the awkwardness of singing along to the television screen, though, while sitting in the living room in our pajamas with the cats chasing one another between naps. My sons barely hummed, and my husband and I tried to be optimistic as we sang through morning voice.

I am thankful, though, for this experience. Not only had I taken for granted the power of being with God's people, but I had also underestimated the power of singing with God's people.

While thy were sandwiched between the Moabites and the Amorites, it wasn't just the water from the well that God would use to refresh His people. It was fellowship and worship, gathering and singing. Not surprisingly, they experienced a great military victory afterward.

NUMBERS: Wisdom as You Worship

What does congregational singing mean to you? How does it refresh your soul?

_____

_____

Do you feel strengthened and restored after being around God's people? Why or why not?

_____

_____

Why do you think it is still so important that God's people gather and sing together?

_____

_____

When have you been able to "win" in life after being strengthened and restored by congregational fellowship and worship?

_____

_____

Wisdom for Worship: Staying Hydrated

Water cleanses. Water sustains. Water strengthens. Water restores. Are we getting the message? Do we fully grasp how desperately we need Christ's Living Water? We thirst daily, and we need Him daily. We cannot thrive as Christians without turning to God to quench our thirst through the atonement that Jesus' death and resurrection provided. We cannot thrive in the Lord's Church without being with and worshiping with His people.

We need cleansing so we can stay near to God. Be thankful for the process of repentance and atonement. Do you regularly confess your sin before the Lord? How so? If not, what keeps you from habitual repentance?

_____

_____

Chapter 8: *Stay Hydrated*

Are Christians sometimes guilty of not repenting enough? Why is this?

_____

_____

Our restoration is nothing short of a miracle. Do not take this for granted! Look up "incarnation." What does this word mean? What is miraculous about the incarnation and its role in our salvation?

_____

_____

Why is it a miracle that YOU are saved through Jesus Christ?

_____

_____

We need to be with one another. Is going to church on Sunday mornings hard for you? Why or why not? What about Sunday nights and midweek Bible classes? Fellowship events? If these come easily for you, why might they be hard for some people to want to attend?

_____

_____

What are some concrete benefits of being with other Christians?

_____

_____

We need to sing with one another. Why do you think God wants us to sing? What is it about corporate singing that makes it so special to God and to us?

_____

_____

How can this worship opportunity be abused in Sunday services?

_____

_____

✦ LESSON 9 ✦

Be Afraid

"'The donkey saw me and turned aside before me these three times. If she had not turned aside from me, surely just now I would have killed you and let her live.'"

(Numbers 22:33)

Before you begin this lesson, answer the following questions.

Do you think of yourself as a fearful person? If so, in what areas?

_____

_____

How can fear be a good thing? When can it be a bad thing?

_____

_____

How easy or difficult is it for you to obey God in a situation where you desperately want to do the OPPOSITE of His will?

_____

_____

Part 1

Numbers 22

Most pet owners appreciate the protective benefits of having dogs, or—yes—even cats, in the house on a regular basis. Some dogs have their watch instincts so sharply tuned that their humans get an alert every time the wind blows, and most breeds show at least some degree of alarm when something is off kilter. Perhaps it's the Amazon Prime driver setting yet another package on your front doorstep, or maybe your dog is used to your frequent purchases and only barks when a delivery person has the audacity to ring the doorbell.

Chapter 9: *Be Afraid*

Ever a defender of cats, I would argue that cats are equally in touch with what is unusual or what may need investigation. I don't agree with all their conclusions—after all, not every empty box my kids set by the trash can carries a lethal threat, thereby warranting full scrutiny by my cats. On more than one occasion, however, I have been home alone and have taken comfort in the fact that ANY unusual noise will be perceived by my cats first; on the other hand, if they don't so much as twitch an ear, then I know that whatever sound I think I heard is normal for our household, for it has not in the least bit disturbed my decidedly judgmental cats.

I have a feeling the king of Moab either had a chihuahua on his front porch or a cat napping nearby—maybe both. When the noise of the Israelites defeating King Og and the Amorites reverberates across the land, Balak knows a stranger is on his front doorstep. The cat looks up in high alert, this time not mocking the typically high-strung chihuahua for overreacting to the rumble they both heard.

When Balak sees a massive army approaching Moab, he panics. This definitely isn't the UPS® driver. He could muster some forces of his own, but his quick assessment is that "they are too mighty for me" (from Numbers 22:6). His cat has run under the bed, and his chihuahua is hysterical by now. Balak consults his staff, ultimately deciding to summon the supernatural.

As we examine Numbers 22, we will see some significant fears and a fair amount of stubbornness as a few people—and even a donkey—encounter God and His people.

Read Numbers 22. What does Balak decide to do, with regard to the problem of the approaching Israelites? (See verses 5-6.)

_____

_____

What did God tell Balaam? (See verse 12.)

_____

_____

What evidence do we see in verses 14-17 that Balak is still very afraid?

_____

_____

NUMBERS: Wisdom as You Worship

What made Balaam's donkey step off the road three times? (See verses 23-27.)

_____

_____

Why is God angry with Balaam? (See verses 22 and 32, also 33.)

_____

_____

At first glance, Balaam's apparent deference to the Lord is impressive. Here is a man who refuses to move or speak without the consent of Jehovah God. Right?

Not exactly. Let's take a closer look.

Balaam was a diviner, a pagan seer who charged a fee for his services (verse 7). I imagine that when Balak's staff arrived, not only with the required fee but also with the evidence of Balak's terror, that Balaam saw an opportunity for gain.

Balak could afford more, and my guess is that Balaam contemplated this for a minute.

It is not within the scope of this lesson to discuss the fascinating dynamics of the One True God speaking to (and, later, through) a pagan prophet; however, He does, and Balaam obeys (verses 12-14), though his motives might be suspect. Notice that Balak's offer advances to include honor and greatness for Balaam if he will—for the love of Pete—get there already and curse the Israelites.

You can almost feel the sweat dripping off Balak's face as he pens a frantic note to Balaam. His fear is palpable; he is desperate. Whatever the prophet wants, the prophet can have.

In anticipation of the bizarre part of this story (God is about to speak through a stinky, hairy donkey), we might read quickly and miss Balaam's misstep. God told Balaam that he could go with Balak's men if they came and knocked on his door again. Given that the men were spending the night, the likelihood is pretty high that they would have certainly come and pestered Balaam again before going back to Moab empty-handed. However, we don't see evidence that they did or that Balaam even waited around long enough to see if they would. What we see (in verse 21) is Balaam simply getting up in the morning and going back with them.

This explains God's anger in verse 22, and let's not dismiss this as petty. God demands our total obedience. Balaam probably thought, *They'll come to me in the morning, so I might as well get up and go.* Likely being both presumptuous and greedy for Balak's reward, Balaam saddles up without waiting to see if God's condition would be met.

This is where Balaam's donkey has more sense than her human. Balaam's donkey sees God and, quite uncharacteristically for her species, will not press forward in stubbornness. Her Maker has blocked the path, and she will not defy Him.

Chapter 9: *Be Afraid*

We know the rest of the story—how stubbornly determined Balaam is to press forward and how angry he gets at the donkey for refusing to do so. God opens the mouth of the donkey and the eyes of Balaam and, in so doing, asserts His sovereignty and His command for obedience. God not-so-gently points out that even the donkey had the sense to fear God.

Balaam seems sufficiently rattled and mildly repentant, and we will soon examine the rest of this story. But for a few minutes, let's examine ourselves and see where we may have a little bit of Balaam in us.

How do you know when you've sinned or when you are close to sinning?

_____

_____

Do you feel genuine fear of God and/or of the sin that can separate you from Him? Why or why not?

_____

_____

Why are Christians sometimes guilty of not having an appropriate fear of the Lord?

_____

_____

What place does the wrath of God have in the gospel message?

_____

_____

The ubiquitous command in Scripture to not be afraid is sometimes inappropriately over-applied to our worship of God. To the point that some believers thoroughly bask in His grace and conveniently dismiss His wrath, sometimes we forget that God is GOD and that He demands complete obedience.

I contend that there are some things of which we need to be quite afraid.

Sin. Distractions. False doctrine. Temptation. Complacency. Idols. Hell.

The list goes on.

Our fear of these things is not rooted in their power, for we are more than conquerors in Christ Jesus (Romans 8:37). Our fear is of what these things can do (lead us away from God) and of what God will do (hold us accountable for them).

I recently heard a wise preacher assert an uncomfortable truth: **The gospel begins with the wrath of God.** Were it not for God's wrath against sin, we would have no need for salvation. God cannot and will not tolerate sin, even from you.

We should be VERY afraid of sin—so much that we are on high alert, just like our pets are, to any inkling that something in our lives is not right.

Part 2
Numbers 23

Recently I read the bestselling book *The Boys in the Boat* by Daniel James Brown, a spectacular memoir of the rowing team that won Olympic Gold in Berlin in 1936. Prior to reading this book, everything I knew about rowing could be written on the top half of a postage stamp. What I know now isn't much more, but one aspect of the sport fascinates me: the role of the coxswain.

In plain language, the coxswain is the taskmaster. He commands the entire boat with demands to slow down, speed up, push harder, pull back—all at keenly discerned moments in a race, so as to outsmart the stamina of the opposing boats.

The coxswain, from what I understand, is the smallest person in the nine-man boat, yet the scope of his authority is impressive to me for two reasons. First, compared to the gargantuan, arachnid limbs synchronized in front of him, he is but a housefly. Second, and maybe most paradoxically, the coxswain doesn't actually row. He barks orders with the fury of a Super Bowl coach in overtime, and he has no mercy for the unbelievable fatigue the oarsmen feel as the finish line to any race draws near. (The winning team's tradition of throwing the coxswain in the water, then, is quite understandable.)

He lacks height, weight, and his own oar, yet every man in the boat obeys him. He is their metronome, their mirror, their sergeant. Their victory depends on him.

The oarsmen have thoroughbred strength, yet they know better than to think for themselves while in the boat. They have one mind, one voice, one strength—and all that rests in the coxswain.

I think of God as a sort of coxswain, ordering the pagan Balaam's every move when it came to His people. Let's return to the story.

Read Numbers 23. Who is putting words in Balaam's mouth?

_____

_____

Chapter 9: *Be Afraid*

What does Balaam have Balak do as he prepares to seek the Lord?

_____

_____

Why is Balak outraged?

_____

_____

What does Balak do to try to get a different result?

_____

_____

Despite his status as a well-known prophet, Balaam acknowledges his own impotence in the presence of God. Copy one of the verses where Balaam speaks of God's authority.

_____

_____

I wonder at the inner turmoil Balaam must have felt during his time with Balak. He was a pagan prophet, a non-Israelite who was not under God's covenant. He was likely a prophet for profit; his divinations were renowned, and he lived a comfortable life in exchange.

Having the sovereign, almighty God usurp his vocal cords, then, cramped his style. To his credit, he seems a bit humbled, and he's probably still fact-checking his own experience with a talking donkey. The Hebrew God clearly has some mojo, and Balaam submits to His authority.

Part 3
Numbers 24

I've seen the video footage probably dozens of times, though when the assassination attempt on President Ronald Reagan actually happened, I don't remember thinking twice about the Secret Service agent who saved the President's life. But the luxury of decades gone by and knowledge of Reagan's survival collectively cherished means we can watch the grainy replays—even in slow motion—and notice minutia instead of reacting in horror.

NUMBERS: Wisdom as You Worship

So the last few times I've seen the footage, I've paid attention to the most fascinating figure in that moment—the member of Reagan's detail who literally took a bullet for the President.

What intrigues me the most is not that he **would** but that he **did**. Sure, that was his job, and sure that was what he was supposed to do. But to the credit of the training, indoctrination, and tenacious methods used to produce Secret Service agents, Agent Tim McCarthy's reaction was lightning-fast, which, incidentally and most fortunately, was faster than the bullet used.

Let's face it. Most of us would hear a bullet being fired and scream, run, hide, grab our kids, and do whatever we could to get out of Dodge. Those are our instincts. But this agent's natural human instincts were completely eclipsed by the influence of his training. Maybe that's even too generous a conjecture. It seems he didn't even have human reflexes anymore, but rather superhuman instincts that were guided by the intentional indoctrination and training of his profession.

You've likely seen the footage yourself, so you know what he did. And what he did was precisely the opposite of what you or I would do during an otherwise routine day at work. He tackled the President, jumping between the gun and the man, with no expectation that he himself wouldn't be harmed or killed.

I'm pretty sure he had a big S on his chest and a red cape underneath his nice suit. Clark Kent probably studied this scene before suiting up for his own day of work.

I'm fascinated by this superhuman ability to put fear and knee-jerk reaction aside and defy expectations by doing the exact opposite thing. Balaam probably didn't share my appreciation for this phenomenon, but he certainly witnessed it. In a perplexing oxymoron, Balaam's fear trumped itself.

Let's read more of this story and consider this.

Read Numbers 24. Why didn't Balaam seek out the typical omens this time?

_____

_____

What did he do instead?

_____

_____

Chapter 9: *Be Afraid*

What caused him to say the complete opposite words that he was hired to say?

_____

_____

How does Balaam himself explain this phenomenon?

_____

_____

Remember that Balaam was a pagan prophet and not a member of God's chosen people. My guess is that his MO was to conveniently receive oracles catered to those willing to pay for favorable outcomes. Balak was counting on this. But Balaam was so overcome by God Himself that he could do nothing but speak the words that the Almighty had put in his mouth.

So where my mind goes now is this: If a pagan prophet can be so overcome by God, surely we can, as people who are heirs to His kingdom! I ask myself, **How can I be so in tune with God that my carnal instincts are completely suppressed by my Christian training?**

The Navy SEALS might be able to answer this. Years ago, the Navy turned to brain science to figure out how they could outwit the amygdala—the brain's hot red panic button. SEALS candidates were failing the program in droves, most of them unable to pass the crucial, notorious "pool comps." To pass pool comps, a SEALS candidate must perform a series of underwater tasks, all while a well-oxygenated instructor is beside them tangling up their breathing equipment, turning off their oxygen supply, unmasking them, tackling them—you get the idea. It's man-to-man combat under at least 8-10 feet of water, with the sole aim of the instructor being to stop the oxygen supply of the SEALS candidate.

The instructor isn't trying to kill the candidate, of course. He is trying to assess the candidate's survival skills in a situation that triggers panic in all living creatures: the fear of drowning.

When they began incorporating brain-based training techniques, the Navy saw an increase in the pass rate for SEALS training. With the completely super-human tasks they are prepared to take on, you can be assured that any member of the Navy SEALS you encounter has learned one thing first and foremost: how to suppress his natural instincts.

So it's possible. It's possible for me to train so hardcore as a soldier for Christ that the tendency to go the way of my flesh is trumped by the fruit of the Spirit. My instinct is to react in anger; the Spirit trains me to be compassionate and forgiving. My instinct is to indulge myself; the Spirit trains me to be self-sacrificing. My instinct is to embrace the world; the Spirit trains me to focus on what is eternal.

What are some natural instincts of yours—ones that don't please God?

_____

_____

What does spiritual training look like? What opportunities for spiritual training are readily available to us?

_____

_____

Of what training can you take advantage to overcome more of your carnal nature?

_____

_____

Wisdom for Worship: Being afraid

The sacrifice of Jesus Christ immerses us in the far-reaching, bottomless love of God. What an unbelievable gift! Let us never stop thanking God for our salvation and the hope of heaven.

A Christian teacher once said that we love celebrating the resurrection, but that maybe we don't contemplate the crucifixion often enough. There is value in meditating on why Christ's sacrifice was necessary. There is value even in **grieving over** the sin in my life and in this world. If I don't shake in my boots when I think about standing before God on Judgment Day, then maybe I am not uncomfortable enough about sin. In the same way I love my children and would do anything to protect them from harm, I must love the Lord enough to fear anything that could damage my proximity to Him.

In the face of approaching evil, we must listen only to the Lord's voice. What are some of the voices we hear in our everyday world? How do they distract us?

_____

_____

Chapter 9: *Be Afraid*

When you see temptation or hardship coming, do you invest more time in God's Word and prayer? Why or why not?

_____
_____

We must embrace God's Word, even when we don't like what it means for us. When have you faced the uncomfortable truth that what you wanted and what God wanted were two different things?

_____
_____

What do we risk if we go our own way, seeking out words we want to hear and not allowing God's Word to convict and correct us?

_____
_____

When we listen to God's voice and obey Him, our sinful nature weakens. What is an area of your life that no longer tempts you or has a grip on you? How has God helped you overcome that?

_____
_____

On what topic would you like to collect Bible verses, so as to build an arsenal of God's Word about a struggle you still face?

_____
_____

⇝ LESSON 10 ⇜

Be Accountable

> "Let the LORD, the God of the spirits of all flesh, appoint a man over the congregation who shall go out before them and come in before them, who shall lead them out and bring them in, that the congregation of the LORD may not be as sheep that have no shepherd."
>
> (Numbers 27:16-17)

Before you begin this lesson, answer the following questions.

What does it mean for a person to be accountable to another?

_____

_____

What is the value of Christians being accountable to each other?

_____

_____

What is difficult about accountable relationships?

_____

_____

Part 1

Numbers 25

My son, Jack, is an avid sports fan, and now that he is the only baby bird left in the nest, so to speak, my husband and I enjoy bonding with him by watching all his favorite teams, as well as their rivals, play. I know absolutely nothing about sports and am as athletic as the chewed-up pencil stub in your second grader's backpack.

Chapter 10: *Be Accountable*

Jack, however, is a good teacher and patiently explains rules, traditions, player stats, and more with me as we follow his teams.

Keeping in mind my limitations, please indulge me as I attempt to recap a somewhat comical, heavily replayed moment on the baseball diamond in July 2021. Anthony Rizzo, at the time playing for the Chicago Cubs, was on third base and should have scored a run when his teammate, Ian Happ, grounded one through the middle.

He didn't.

Instead, he says he "froze," uncharacteristically. He started to run, then hesitated, then turned back toward third base, then went back toward home, and so on. To my untrained eye, it simply looked like a game of Monkey in the Middle. That was the humorous part.

The fascinating part was the reaction of the players on the infield, who were all blazing in from their various positions to cover every inch of the baseline with the assurance that Rizzo wouldn't score. As Rizzo went back and forth like a poor, confused squirrel in the middle of a highway, the St. Louis Cardinals were passing the ball from one to the next, back to the one, then again to the next, in a near-linear formation instead of a diamond. Anyone who didn't know the players or the game well (like me) couldn't tell the difference between the first baseman, second baseman, third baseman, short stop, pitcher, or catcher because they were all playing in a line with no regard for the part of the field they usually work.

By the time that one play was over, all six infield players had touched the ball at least once, some twice. It was crazy to watch!

What absolutely amazed me was the lightning-fast reflexes of every single player on the field. The play took only a few seconds. There was clearly one goal: get Rizzo out. Everyone with a red bird on his shirt was responsible to make that happen, no matter which part of the diamond they normally covered.

I think Aaron's grandson, Phinehas, might appreciate this moment in sports. If there is wi-fi in Paradise, perhaps he's even enjoyed the replay, permanently cataloged in the vaults of YouTube. Phinehas didn't play for the Cardinals, but this work ethic would have been a good example.

Let's watch Phinehas's big play for God as we read on in Numbers.

Read Numbers 25. In what egregious sins did the people of Israel engage?

_____

_____

NUMBERS: Wisdom as You Worship

Describe how one Israelite blatantly and openly participated in this. (See verse 6.)

_____
_____

What was Phinehas's reaction upon witnessing this?

_____
_____

How does God reflect on Phinehas's "play" for Him?

_____
_____

With Phinehas playing for Team Jehovah God, there was clearly one goal: get sin out. Everyone with Hebrew DNA was responsible to make that happen, even if it meant holding one of their own accountable.

Or, in this case, even if it meant grabbing a sword and stabbing a fellow teammate and his lover through their entwined bodies as they unashamedly had sex in the Israelite's own bedroom.

Ouch.

That might be why Phinehas's actions are so honored by God. Not only was he zealous for God—a state of heart I pray is true of me—but he did the uncomfortable thing. The awkward thing. The might-cost-you-a-few-friendships thing.

Recently, a friend came up to me with blatant gossip. She even bent inward as she shared this information, and I was aware in that moment that the conversation was sin. She is a Christian, so I also knew that I had an obligation to silence her so that sin did not further grip her (and me).

I'm ashamed to say that I chickened out.

I thought of the situation and made excuses about the timing—how it wasn't a good moment to try to confront her because we were in the middle of a busy task. I made the excuse inside myself that she should know better and that the Holy Spirit would surely convict her without my help. I also worried that she would get mad at me and that our relationship would be thereafter strained.

I guess my inaction could be attributed somewhat to my personality (introvert, peacemaker), but more than likely just flat-out lack of courage and zeal. I would rather be corrected than correct another.

Chapter 10: *Be Accountable*

So maybe I'm the only one for whom accountability between Christians is sometimes incredibly hard, but I'm guessing there are many of you who can relate. But we can't let ourselves be strengthened by the numbers of us who are sheepish about confrontation. Paul urged the Galatians to restore brothers and sisters in Christ who are in sin (6:1), and his messages to other churches repeatedly addressed the need to get sin out of their congregations (all with the goal of restoring the sinner, of course).

If you have ever been corrected by another Christian, how did that moment go?

_____

_____

What are important things to keep in mind when confronting fellow Christians about their sin?

_____

_____

Have you ever confronted another Christian in their sin? How did that moment go?

_____

_____

How can we be more courageous and zealous in protecting the Lord's Church from the infiltration of sin?

_____

_____

Part 2

Numbers 26

There's a lot of counting involved as Israel conducts another census, but this census involves some key players. This census tallies the number of new-generation Israelites, so these are the ones who will literally enter Canaan. (Their parents will die before they get there, remember.)

Like the last time, they'll count the able-bodied men, "all in Israel who are able to go to war" (verse 2). Let's see how this turned out for them.

NUMBERS: Wisdom as You Worship

Read Numbers 26. Who was in charge of this census?

_____

_____

Complete the table below with the numbers they reported.

Tribe	Total in Number
Reuben	
Simeon	
Gad	
Judah	
Issachar	
Zebulun	
Joseph: Manasseh	
Joseph: Ephraim	
Benjamin	
Dan	
Asher	
Naphtali	
Total	

Chapter 10: *Be Accountable*

They would have emerged from the desert as a slightly larger nation had they not had their rendezvous with the women and the gods of Moab. Their sin came with the hefty price tag of a deadly plague; 24,000 Israelites fell to God's wrath.

I'm sure there were some who offered to apologize. Probably many who promised never to do it again. The consequences were irrevocable, though, and God had to purge sin from their camp once again.

So when the new census is complete, they are somewhat fewer in number than when they began, a reality that may or may not have rattled those who knew. Given that they were moving forward to usurp the land of Canaan, numbers were pretty important when it came to able-bodied warriors.

We see another consequence of sin in this chapter, one creeping up 40 years after the fact. Like a child who hopes his mother will forget about the spanking she's promised he'll get "when we get home," I wonder if even Moses was hoping God might ease up on His promise that none of the first generation would live to see "when we get home." With the exception of Caleb and Joshua, verse 65 confirms that God, in fact, did remember the spanking He promised, so to speak.

Let's not forget that sin keeps a predictable course. We are forgiven through the blood of Jesus Christ, but we live in the natural world, and God does not exempt us from its harsh realities. Like our own children sometimes, we want "sorry" or "I won't do it again" to be enough. But the point is simply this: The choices we make have short-term consequences and long-term impact.

Give an example from you or the world around you in which the cost of sin left someone weakened for the battles ahead.

_____

_____

Give an example in which the consequences of sin showed up a long time after the sin itself.

_____

_____

What does this teach us about accountability in our spiritual lives?

_____

_____

NUMBERS: Wisdom as You Worship

Part 3
Numbers 27

You can almost feel the anticipation building among the people. The Promised Land is really a thing, and it's so near they can almost taste it—except, of course, they won't. Their children will, however, and most of us can understand the passion with which parents work on behalf of their children.

Numbers 27 begins with a concern that will be further fleshed out in a later chapter, and I love the glimpse we get here of the tender care God has for women. The chapter ends with Moses' paternal plea for those who followed him.

Read Numbers 27. Who approaches Moses in verses 1-4? What is their concern?

_____

_____

What does Moses do before he answers them?

_____

_____

What is God's response to this dilemma?

_____

_____

Knowing his death was near, what was Moses' passionate plea to God on behalf of the children of Israel?

_____

_____

As Moses' life nears its end, God reminds Moses that he can see the Promised Land from a distance but may never enter it. God reminds Moses of his sin at Meribah, though I'm not sure this is God's rubbing it in. I wonder if, instead, God's heart was heavy with sadness that His chosen leader could not enter Canaan.

To his credit, Moses did not argue with God. He didn't whine, "Come on, Lord, that was **years** ago. Seriously? I've been with them from Day 1."

Chapter 10: *Be Accountable*

Instead, he pleaded with God to keep His people in His care by appointing another leader over them. After 40 long years with this ragtag congregation of chosen people, Moses had learned a thing or two about accountability.

There's a casual quip in pop culture that would probably make Moses burn his beard. "You do you" is the most common iteration, with the general message being that each person is encouraged to live according to his or her own plan and desires and beliefs.

Moses' late-in-life prayer, though, counters this toxic maxim. **"Let the Lord, the God of the spirits of all flesh, appoint a man over the congregation…that the congregation of the Lord may not be as sheep that have no shepherd"** (vs. 16-17). Probably understanding that the wandering, fickle, prone-to-compromise people of Israel were representative of the tendencies in "the spirits of all flesh," Moses prayed for leadership that would provide rules, direction, and supervision.

It's easy for us to appreciate why Israel needed a leader; after all, we've read their story. We are removed from it, in a literal sense, so we are not imposing a mayor on our own town, so to speak, to cheer on the inauguration of Joshua.

But how do we respond to rules and leadership in our worlds? The homeowners' association in your neighborhood? The cop who just pulled you over for speeding? Your boss at work? Elders at church? Your spouse?

The truth is that we need rules. We need leadership. We even need people to call us out. It's not fun, but if our commitment to living in covenant with Christ and His Church is sincere, we should ultimately welcome anything or anybody who forces us to shed the weight of sin.

Who are the hardest people in your life to whom you submit?

_____

_____

How do leaders even in the secular world help us stay on God's path?

_____

_____

For whom are you a leader? Do you inspire people to live more righteously? Reflect on your influence on those around you.

_____

_____

Wisdom for Worship: Being Accountable

You can't do this on your own. God's design for His people is that we live in fellowship with one another—helping, loving. and upholding one another. Sometimes this involves uncomfortable conversations, and sometimes this may hurt deeply. Ultimately, our proximity to God depends on our distance from sin, but this sin is sometimes hard to see before we are buried in it. We need one another! Carefully monitoring our own spiritual health with humility and meekness, we must help others stay on the path to heaven by guarding against sin and obeying the teachings of Christ.

God loves us enough to have the hard conversations and the awkward moments. What kind of relationship is the foundation for His love for us?

_____

_____

How can we build this kind of relationship with others so that accountability works more authentically?

_____

_____

Keep track of your numbers. Are you watching future generations? What is the strength level of the youth in your congregation?

_____

_____

Why is it important to continuously monitor the number of young people in the Church?

_____

_____

Chapter 10: *Be Accountable*

Follow the leaders. What situations could we perhaps navigate better if we went to our elders and asked for help and guidance?

_____

_____

What issues do you encounter in your daily life about which you need to remember to consult leaders (your husband, your boss, etc.)?

_____

_____

✦ LESSON 11 ✦

Make the Time

*"These you shall offer to the L***ORD** *at your appointed feasts, in addition to your vow offerings and your freewill offerings, for your burnt offerings, and for your grain offerings, and for your drink offerings, and for your peace offerings."*

(Numbers 29:39)

Before you begin this lesson, answer the following questions.

How often do you worship God?

_____

_____

Why do you worship God?

_____

_____

When is worshiping God hard for you?

_____

_____

Part 1
Numbers 28

I love flowers, and I have grand aspirations for a beautifully manicured curb appeal to our house. On my daily walks around the neighborhood, I absolutely love looking at the flower beds and landscaping of the houses on each street. I imagine all the plants and flowers that would look nice in my yard, and I've even occasionally done internet searches on which indoor plants would be nontoxic to cats. Indoor plants add life to a home, so wouldn't it be grand to have them in our kitchen and by the windows?

Chapter 11: *Make the Time*

Alas, I'm a terrible plant mom. The only plants I can keep alive are fake ones. Green thumbs are prominent among the women in my family, but they climbed out of the gene pool to towel off and eat a sandwich when my DNA was constructed. I have absolutely zero instinct for their care. Many women in my family just know where in their yards or homes a plant would thrive, and they have flawless taste in choosing just the right species to group together or spread apart.

So I don't represent well. I would rather provide neonatal care to a litter of hamsters for a week than to be in charge of my dear friend's plants while she's on vacation. The thing that seems to get me is the daily-ness of plant care. Water or don't water—and how much water? Enough to drench the soil or just dampen it? Sunshine all day, every day, or just in the mornings? Miracle-Gro® or no?

Every. Single. Day.

My plant friends argue that cat care is a daily thing, too, but at least cats can make their needs known. Plants just sit there expecting you to know what they need, and then all of a sudden they die if you've failed to figure it out.

But in a way, this is a powerful lesson to us spiritually. Before we unpack it, though, let's read on in Numbers.

Read Numbers 28. How does God describe the offerings in verses 6, 10, 15, 24, and 31?

_____

_____

What was the purpose of these offerings?

_____

_____

What would God's reaction be to these offerings?

_____

_____

What is the context of these instructions from God to Moses (see chapter 27, verse 13)?

_____

_____

NUMBERS: Wisdom as You Worship

In short, before Moses dies, God has him remind the people of Israel to go to church every Sunday—in the Old Testament sense, that is. Regular worship was commanded by God. Some of the offerings were weekly, some were annual, but all happened on a regular schedule.

The Bible class my husband and I attend on Sunday mornings has often discussed the stealth of Satan in turning one of COVID's greatest blessings into a parachute by which one can slowly fall away from God. During COVID quarantines, many of us enjoyed the blessing of weekly "online church" that modern technology made fairly easy for most congregations to provide. Though we certainly would have preferred in-person hugs and singing with dozens of others instead of by ourselves, online church made a way for God's people to still gather (sort of) and worship Him every Sunday.

Now that the technology kinks of live broadcasts are worked through, most congregations continue to offer online church even though in-person worship has resumed. This blesses our shut-ins and those who are still quarantining or otherwise unable to attend worship on a given Sunday.

This blessing comes with a warning label endorsed by Satan himself, however, and can be taken for granted when our winter flannel sheets and our cozy bunny slippers feel better than getting dressed for church. Watching from the living room is easier than getting everyone in the house ready, out the door, and in the church building on time for classes and worship. And for the overworked, tired, and/or introverted among us, watching church online is easier than "people-ing" on a day when we just want to rest before another week begins.

I totally get this. In fact, my entire household gets this. Like many of you, our calendars are bigger than our reserve of energy most days, and—to be frank—during COVID lockdown, we really enjoyed sleeping a tad bit longer and sliding into the recliners with coffee and our afghans on Sunday mornings.

What is the danger in choosing to watch church from home instead of joining others in study and worship each week? You have probably met some Christians who actually don't see much danger at all in this approach, but Scripture calls us to be together, and for good reason.

On a pure obedience level, Christians are commanded to "not [neglect] to meet together, as is the habit of some" (Hebrews 10:25). We are also called to "restore" each other when we are in sin and "bear one another's burdens" (Galatians 6:1-2). We are to "rejoice with those who rejoice" and "weep with those who weep" (Romans 12:15). How can we do this if we are not building relationships and seeing each other regularly?

I fear that those who are content with watching church on TV are sidestepping these responsibilities and, as a result, walking in disobedience even as they sit on their couch.

Chapter 11: *Make the Time*

What are some ways people justify not needing to be in church each week to be able to thrive in their Christian lives?

_____

_____

What are common excuses for missing church?

_____

_____

What about Sunday evening worship and midweek Bible classes? What do you think Scripture teaches us about those additional gatherings?

_____

_____

What should we teach our children (and use as a guideline for ourselves) about "when it's okay to miss church" and/or "when it's okay to watch online"?

_____

_____

Part 2
Numbers 29

Our family calendar tends to have a "feast or famine" appearance to it. In July alone, we recognize five birthdays and one anniversary. The stretch from Halloween through Christmas is equally clustered (and expensive), with six birthdays and two major holidays.

Despite the rotund nature of these months, I don't recall that we've ever chosen to forego a birthday or holiday celebration because we were too busy or too tired. We certainly don't have big parties for every special occasion, but we always acknowledge them in some way. Gifts, cakes, dinners, decorations, or special photos taken send the loud message that these people and these occasions are special to us—sacred, even, in that families and our memories with them are among God's greatest blessings.

The people and occasions that make up the Lord's Church are equally important, and we get hints of this in Numbers as God sets up an online calendar for the Israelites. Let's look at a few of these special times.

NUMBERS: Wisdom as You Worship

Read Numbers 29. If your translation has section titles, write out how this chapter is divided.

_____

_____

What were the people commanded *not to do* during these special occasions?

_____

_____

What were the people commanded *to do* during these special occasions?

_____

_____

Catherine "Kitty" Genovese was on her way home from work one early spring morning of 1964 when she was brutally stabbed, raped, and robbed by a seemingly random man on the New York City sidewalk, near Kitty's apartment building in Queens. Apparently, someone heard or saw the commotion and yelled out a window to leave this woman alone, but that only scared the murderer off for a few minutes before he returned to Kitty, who was collapsed and bleeding at the bottom of the staircase leading to her apartment. He finished the evil he'd started, and he left the scene. Kitty was soon discovered, and she died in the ambulance on the way to the hospital.

This story was sensationalized at the time it happened. The longstanding focus of the media's enthusiasm for this news story was what became known as "the bystander effect." Though many came to dismiss the initial reports as falsified rumors with no evidence (except to the contrary), the general uproar surrounding Kitty's murder involved the alleged inaction of what were surely multiple witnesses. How could so many people see a woman get attacked and do absolutely nothing?

Psychologists at the time weighed in, explaining the influence of numbers. The bystander effect is simply this: People are less likely to act when there are plenty of others who appear to be acting or are presumed to be acting. If I see a car have a wreck, but I notice that plenty of other cars are even closer to the accident than I am, I am likely to dismiss my responsibility to call 911 because surely all these other people will take care of that. Though most finally conceded that there couldn't have been many witnesses at all to the murder of Kitty Genovese, the psychological phenomenon that emerged from the initial gossip and false reporting remains commonplace today.

Chapter 11: *Make the Time*

I'm concerned that there may be hints of the bystander effect in the Church today, especially regarding worship and service to the Lord. Whether your congregation consists of 50 people or 500, you might see that in some ways, it can be easy for people to remain in the background. Plenty of women are on the church nursery rotation schedule, for example, so I don't need to volunteer. Several boys and men facilitate the Sunday service, so my son doesn't need to sign up to help. Myriad crockpots full of tasty food are set out on the folding tables in the gym, so I don't need to bring anything for the potluck. Dozens of people are singing right now, so I don't need to offer up my voice. Most of the congregation gives financially, so I don't need to make a contribution.

In short, my worship might be missing the crucial component of sacrifice if I am content to sit back on my haunches and only serve the Lord when I get the notion to do so. During the special times of worship we read about in Numbers 29, God commanded the Israelites to avoid work; instead, this worship was all about making sacrifices to the Lord. What if I see plenty of people around me engaging in worship and service to the Lord, so I let go of my responsibility to do the same? Instead, I work for myself and pad my spiritual ego with an occasional monetary gift or a meal brought to a friend in need—on my schedule and within my comfort zone.

I've re-read Numbers 29 to see if God exempts any of His people from ritual worship. He doesn't. That means you and I need to take personal responsibility for ours, no matter how many people around us seem to be making Him happy.

Where do you think the bystander effect might be most common in churches?

_____

_____

Have you ever held back in church ministry because there seemed to be plenty of people who were doing a particular job?

_____

_____

When a ministry is legitimately well-volunteered, what should we do to avoid spiritual idleness?

_____

_____

During singing, prayer, and Bible reading, do you sacrifice your mind to the Lord and discipline yourself to only meditate on Him? What makes this hard?

___

___

Part 3
Numbers 30

It's been over three years since my younger son, Jack, had an accident while tubing behind a boat on Kentucky Lake. Bouncing off the tube and slamming "just so" into a wake, he shattered his femur and was gingerly transported to the local hospital by volunteer paramedics.

His injury was severe; his femoral artery was throbbing precariously close to shards of bone that could sever it at any moment, causing a life-threatening loss of blood. The local hospital threw up their hands and cried "uncle," referring him to the nearest hospital with a Level 1 Pediatric Trauma Center. There wasn't time for an ambulance to make the 3+ hour transport, so he had to be air-lifted via medical helicopter.

LeBonheur Children's Hospital in Memphis, as well as the talented surgeon who treated Jack, were AMAZING. We thanked God profusely for their watchful care over Jack and their compassion for us during his hospital stay.

The hospital was phenomenal, but it was also out-of-network. And the helicopter crew doesn't waste time photocopying insurance cards, so my husband and I knew to expect a bill directly from the med-evac company. We would have to take the bill to our insurance company for help with payment.

My husband is extremely wise and scrupulous with money, so once he knew Jack would make a full recovery, he started sweating about the bills that would be coming in—likely making it to our mailbox before we even got home from the hospital. The out-of-network hospital charges might be authorized since no other hospital in the area could treat Jack, but we had no idea what to expect with the helicopter bill. My husband Googled the average cost of medical air transport and tried to brace himself for a bill that would—according to Google's estimation—likely be around $10,000.

Turns out, Google was off by a few dollars. The helicopter transport bill came in at over $68,000! Add to that the out-of-network hospital charges, surgery fees, hardware charges (the titanium screws put in his leg cost approximately $2,000 each), countless physical therapy visits, etc. The final result?

Not. One. Single. Cent.

Chapter 11: *Make the Time*

That's right. My husband and I were not required to pay even one dollar for Jack's entire ordeal! I wanted to celebrate and move on, but my husband was dubious, as it seemed too good to be true that we wouldn't owe even a dime—not to the hospital, not for the helicopter, not to the surgeon, not to our insurance company. Nothing. So he bravely called the insurance company, fully expecting an explanation for why the medical bills for Jack's accident all of a sudden stopped coming in.

But it was true! The insurance company paid 100% of the charges associated with Jack's accident, including the helicopter bill. Though we would have signed over our house to do whatever it took to get Jack medical treatment, we'd been beyond nervous about the monstrous charges accruing during those first several days. It was like we'd snuck the insurance company's credit card out of their wallet and went on a shopping spree without their permission.

And then it was like they said—in a rare, amazingly simple process—"Oh, good, we're glad you found the credit card. We got it."

I don't have to tell you that insurance companies can be notoriously difficult to work with, but in this instance they did exactly what they were intended to do: In a medical crisis where costs were extreme, they stepped up and footed the bill for their client.

Some women may find Numbers 30 slightly off putting at first read. We'll see why in a second, but before we read, I'd like to encourage us to keep the example of the insurance company as a framework by which to process God's placement of women under the authority of men.

Read Numbers 30. For whom is God looking out in this chapter?

_____

_____

If the woman/girl is unmarried, who is responsible for managing her vows?

_____

_____

If the woman/girl is married, who is responsible for managing her vows?

_____

_____

NUMBERS: Wisdom as You Worship

How is God's compassion and care for women evident in this chapter?

_____

_____

Twentieth-century anthropologist Margaret Mead spent decades studying ancient, primitive cultures. There is some debate as to whether the following continued conversation on a broken femur can be attributed to her or was embellished by ambitious scholars reporting on her work. I'm not sure if the following thoughts are original to Mead, but having been through the intense trauma of my son's injury, however, I can absolutely believe in the principle behind them.

According to some, Mead was allegedly asked what the first sign of civilization is in any given culture. Mead (or whoever embellished her findings) answered that a healed femur bone was indicative of a culture that had segued from barbarism to civility. The rationale is this: The femur is the hardest, most painful bone in the body to break. A person cannot simply ignore it and hope it gets well on its own. In contrast, if a femur has healed, this means that someone has provided help and support for the lengthy healing ahead; otherwise, a person or animal with a broken femur would simply be left for dead, prone to be the next night's dinner for area carnivores. When people reach out and uphold one another during hard times, the foundation for civility is formed.

When I read Numbers 30, I see God giving women a large insurance policy—one that will protect her in a crisis. God is putting in place those whose job it is to provide support and help for any women who break their femurs, so to speak, and in this way, He is ensuring they are safe, provided for, and cared for.

What a beautiful gift to us!

What do you think "vows" look like in our modern culture, apart from marriage vows?

_____

_____

In what way does God provide for our protection during times of trouble?

_____

_____

Chapter 11: *Make the Time*

Speak to the investment of time that it means to come alongside someone who is in trouble.

_____

_____

How is supporting a fellow Christian during hardship an example of worship to God?

_____

_____

Wisdom for Worship: Making the Time

Time might be our most valued commodity in 21st century American culture. We might even be more prone to protect our time than we do our wallets, especially when it comes to worship. King David captured the essence of sacrificial worship when he refused to offer the Lord animals that he didn't have to pay for: "But the king said to Araunah, 'No, but I will buy it from you for a price. I will not offer burnt offerings to the Lord my God that cost me nothing.' So David bought the threshing floor and the oxen for fifty shekels of silver" (2 Samuel 24:24).

Maybe you're generous with your time, but I suspect many of us squirm a little when we must give up a much-loved activity to be able to invest time in worship and service to the Lord. There is something so incredibly holy, though, about a teenager who refuses to practice his sport or play in any games that pull him away from church attendance. There is something sacred about a busy, tired mom who willingly teaches the three-year-olds' class on Sunday mornings. There is a quieting beauty in the widow who still attends baby showers and bridal showers for the women in the congregation.

If you weren't doing this Bible study right now, you'd be doing something else. Whether a fun game on your phone, a must-see series on Netflix, or a long overdue nap on the couch, there is plenty of competition for your time and for mine. Do we have a godly perspective of our daily schedules?

Let's consider a few lessons from this section of Numbers.

NUMBERS: Wisdom as You Worship

We need to go to church. How can you answer a believer who thinks that attending church isn't necessary?

Would your explanation to a non-Christian be any different? How would you explain the value of church attendance to someone who isn't a Christian?

Other people are doing it, but we still need to do it, too. How are some people able to remain anonymous, so to speak, in a congregation? How is this dangerous to the Church at large?

How can we encourage other "bystanders" to join in and worship and serve with us?

If we call ourselves Christians, then we must give our calendars to God. For whom do you think this is hardest? Why?

What might be the value of "soul searching" with one's calendar in hand? What spiritual (and other) blessings might result in this kind of meditation?

Chapter 11: *Make the Time*

❋ LESSON 12 ❋

Clean House

"But if you do not drive out the inhabitants of the land from before you, then those of them whom you let remain shall be as barbs in your eyes and thorns in your sides, and they shall trouble you in the land where you dwell."

(Numbers 33:55)

Before you begin this lesson, answer the following questions.

What part of your house is most important to you to keep clean? What part do you not mind being messy or cluttered? What's the difference in these two spaces?

_____

_____

What is something that others might throw away but you prefer to keep? What is something that you tend to throw away but someone else might want to salvage?

_____

_____

What do you know about wound care—even for minor scrapes and cuts? What can that teach us in our spiritual lives?

_____

_____

Chapter 12: *Clean House*

Part 1
Numbers 31

I have a blood disorder that required a splenectomy last summer. A person can live a relatively normal life without a spleen; however, there are certain bacteria that the body cannot fight without one. My layperson's, overly simplified explanation is this: Encapsulated bacteria must be dismantled by one's spleen, so the body can attack them properly when they enter the bloodstream. Without a spleen to strip these diseases down first, the remaining players on the body's defense will be overcome by them.

Thanks to modern medicine, the easy solution for those who need their spleen removed is preemptive vaccines against the Big Three: *Streptococcus pneumoniae, Haemophilus influenzae,* and *Neisseria meningitidis*. Accordingly, two weeks before my surgery, I went to my hematologist's office for the three shots.

Now spleenless and appropriately vaccinated, my body is no longer vulnerable to the three diseases that could kill me. Though there are other precautions I must take in an illness, the "biggies" have been stonewalled.

I'm intrigued by the spiritual metaphor this could be. As fallen people, we are vulnerable to sin that kills. What kinds of spiritual vaccines, so to speak, can we take to proactively (and prophylactically) build up our ability to fight off the disease of sin?

Unfortunately, the Israelites do not appear to have gone to the Shot Nurse to preempt their temptations for lust and idolatry.

Read Numbers 31. Why did the Lord sic the Israelites on Midian?

_____

_____

Which pagan prophet did the Israelites kill in this raid?

_____

_____

Why was Moses angry with the army officers?

_____

_____

NUMBERS: Wisdom as You Worship

What had these women done to the Israelites? Whose advice were they following when they did this?

_____

_____

Sometimes we walk right into sin with full knowledge of what we're doing. Maybe there's outright rebellion in our hearts. Maybe we're indulging ourselves, with dangerously presumptuous plans to beg for forgiveness later. Maybe we're apathetic. Maybe we're tired. Bored. Curious.

Other times, however, we are deceived. We are enticed, duped into a situation we thought was benign, only to step into the quicksand of sin the second we let our guards down. Are we still at fault? You betcha. Leviticus makes clear that even unintentional sin is still sin.

How could anyone NOT sin in that situation? we may wonder as we contemplate, and perhaps attempt to defend, our own weakness. King David pondered this, too: "How can a young man keep his way pure? By guarding it according to your word" (Psalm 119:9).

Did you catch that? We are to intentionally guard against sin using the parameters of God's Word. Maybe it's also worth noting what is NOT part of the answer to the question:

> **Just do the best you can.**
> **Follow your heart. You'll know what's right. Do what feels right.**
> **Play it by ear, as each situation is different.**

None of this advice is scriptural, and none of it is the answer to the pertinent question of how to avoid sin. There is ONE answer to that question, and David gave it to us succinctly.

What sins do you find yourself walking right into at times?

_____

_____

Do you blame others, or are you quick to own up to your sin? Explain.

_____

_____

Chapter 12: *Clean House*

What Bible verse can you memorize as a "vaccine" to help you guard against your problem-area sins?

_____

_____

Part 2

Numbers 32

We probably all know what it's like to watch someone "settle." We have likely all "settled" in one way or another. Though secular humanism would urge us to "never settle for less than what you deserve," there are probably plenty of areas where settling has benign consequences. You walk into an ice cream store craving Rocky Road, but, alas, they are out of it, so you settle for Chocolate Delight. You have always wanted a red car, but the price tag on the white car is better, so you settle for it.

Completely harmless. Or, possibly, even beneficial.

Other sacrifices may come with a twinge of sadness or even pronounced grief. You've always wanted a large family, but your husband has put his foot down after one child. You grew up dreaming of becoming a psychologist, but the lengthy years of schooling had more patience than your bank account did.

Uncomfortable with the kind of pain that requires the Healer, the world discourages any decisions that distract us from our dreams and longings. Pursue anything and everything that will make you happy and fulfill you!

Or so they say.

Ironically, this relentless pursuit of self-actualization is far-removed from the only authentic Source of abundance in this life—Jesus Christ. **Settling** for the **less-than-abundant** life that He offers is a bigger conversation than Mississippi Mud vs. Cookies 'n Cream. Sadly, when we align our thinking with the world around us, we end up believing that nothing is more important than our desires, dreams, and goals. Self-sacrifice is not only frowned upon but warned against—as if I am in danger of living a depressed, miserable life if I settle for anything less than what I want.

This clashes, naturally, with life in Jesus Christ, Who calls us to give up and give of ourselves to serve His Church and the lost. But we're getting several centuries ahead of ourselves.

Let's look at some people who were on the brink of the very Promised Land itself, yet still preferred a space that appealed to their own desires.

NUMBERS: Wisdom as You Worship

Read Numbers 32. What did the tribes of Reuben and Gad (and the half-tribe of Manasseh) want, instead of land across the Jordan River?

___

Why did they want this land?

___

Why did this upset Moses?

___

What compromise did they reach?

___

What was Moses' firm warning to them?

___

I would like to learn more about this apparent compromise. First Chronicles 5 makes it clear that Reuben and Gad kept their promise to fight with Israel, yet there is a twinge of sadness as Reuben's egregious sin of incest seems to have led to this distance between them and the other tribes.

This makes me think of the challenge that the COVID pandemic has brought to Christians. Though online worship was, thankfully, widely available to many of us, the foothold Satan appears to have seized is apparent through this same technology.

Chapter 12: *Clean House*

After months of worshiping from their living rooms, some Christians came to prefer the comfort of watching church on TV in their pajamas. There are a host of blessings we miss when we are not physically present with the people of God, but Numbers 32 sheds light on another propensity that physical distance could have: a lack of follow-through and action in our faith. If we habitually disconnect from a body of believers, we are much more vulnerable to losing our strength for spiritual battle, among other things.

You've probably seen at least a minute or two of the television show *Hoarders*. Or maybe, like me, you have lived that nightmare with a family member who suffered with the mental illness that drives one to live in extreme clutter, filth, and mess. A sad part of this condition is the **isolation** that hoarders experience.

Most of them live alone, never having company or visitors—unless you count the many varmints that live quite bountifully in the houses of hoarders. In fact, many hoarders never even have anyone ride in their cars with them because their cars are usually as dangerously cluttered as their homes are; no one else can even fit in the vehicle. Isolation protects them from having to face the reality of the illness and the danger because as soon as a family member, a property manager, or a police officer opens their front door, they are confronted with the reality that there is a serious problem.

Staying away from "in-person" church might lead to a similar condition—a state of spiritual decay, where we are so isolated from Christians that we never confront the sin that is infecting our lives. We never have to clean up, so to speak, and we become fertile environments for spiritual vermin.

What was it like for you to experience the isolation of COVID, particularly from the people of God?

When are you tempted to distance yourself from physical fellowship with other Christians?

Have you ever seen your soul suffer from distance between you and the Church? Explain.

NUMBERS: Wisdom as You Worship

Part 3
Numbers 33

This chapter is a recap of Israel's itinerary since leaving Egypt. If they were applying for a car loan or a mortgage, this transience would be a nightmare to list, definitely requiring extra paper. Though a straightforward list of where they went and where they went next, God's hand on them is evident even in this record. Let's pay special attention to these references as we read on.

Read Numbers 33. Who wrote this record?

_____

_____

Upon whom did God also "execute judgment," according to verse 4? What do you think this looked like?

_____

_____

What kind of refreshment did God provide them at Elim (see verse 9)?

_____

_____

What happened as God's people neared Canaan? (Look at verse 40.)

_____

_____

Before we yawn our way through the first 49 verses of this chapter, let's recall the reason for most of it. Most of this back-and-forth, seemingly pointless wandering was a consequence of, not surprisingly, sin.

Chapter 12: *Clean House*

Remember Numbers 14? The spies' reports and the people's bitter response to them? They scored 40 years in the wilderness for their rebellion and grumbling. So as soporific as the travel itinerary in chapter 33 is, the value in recounting it extends beyond mere recordkeeping. I imagine there was some deep sorrow and regret in Moses' heart as he penned this passage. All the arrows from here to there, then down to there and over to there—the years when even Siri® gave up on them for all the recalculating—were stark reminders of their sin.

So the gut-job instructions from God as Priority #1 when they get across the Jordan make sense, then. This would not be a turnkey, move-in-ready real estate transaction. Instead, this would be flip or flop. Literally.

Either they completely level Canaan, or they'd perpetually face serious hardship. And what would be the first to take the sledgehammer on Demo Day? You guessed it, probably before you even read it in verse 52. Idols. Worship centers. Asherim. Images. **Anything** connected to pagan religion. Get. It. Out. COMPLETELY.

Let's not miss this powerful lesson for Christians today. We cannot nurture the hope of heaven if we accommodate sin.

What might be considered modern-day idols, images, and Asherim?

_____

_____

How are "gods" disguised in American culture?

_____

_____

What would it look like for a Christian to identify and destroy one of these idols in her life?

_____

_____

Wisdom for Worship: Cleaning House

Quite simply, God may not like the way you've decorated your house. I mean this symbolically, though it's quite possible there are physical items in your home that need to be trashed so that you may honor our One True God. What have you "decorated" your life with, though? Where do you perhaps accommodate sin? Which icons or habits of modern culture have you embraced? How have these become idols in your life?

These are hard questions to think about and even harder to answer honestly. Distance from our brothers and sisters in Christ means we don't have these kinds of soul-makeovers as often as we should. I pray we can absorb the things God would have us to learn from His Word, even from parts of Scripture that may seem, at first glance, to be mere historical records. Here are a few take-aways from this section of Numbers.

God reigns, and He casts down paganism. How does this truth contrast with modern religious messages?

_____

_____

What tidbits of paganism exist in your traditions, habits, or possessions? What would God have you to do with this?

_____

_____

We are better off if we surrender our idols ourselves! Remind yourself what an idol is. Why are idols so dangerous for our spiritual lives?

_____

_____

Chapter 12: *Clean House*

What can Christians do to become more adept at recognizing and tearing down idols in our lives?

_____
_____

Distance from God's people makes us vulnerable to sin. How can we answer those who claim to be Christians but say they don't need to be in church?

_____
_____

What cautions should we take in the Church as technology makes "virtual" experiences possible for nearly every activity?

_____
_____

✤ LESSON 13 ✤

Leave an Inheritance

"Command the people of Israel to give to the Levites some of the inheritance of their possession as cities for them to dwell in."
(Numbers 35:2)

Before you begin this lesson, answer the following questions.

Do you have special heirlooms that are passed down in your family? What are they? Who gets them?

What kinds of traditions are important to you in your family?

What do you think of when people talk about "boundaries" in relationships?

Chapter 13: *Leave an Inheritance*

Part 1
Numbers 34

I am probably over-reaching here, but I find it intriguing that water helped delineate boundaries in all four cardinal directions of the Promised Land. It's probably mere, benign coincidence. But God's constant reminders to His people—both the present generation of Israelites and the future members of the Lord's Church—of their means of salvation seem to point consistently back to water.

God had delivered the Israelites through water, and now He was using water to help hem them in to their new land.

At the very least, though, God clearly indicated where their land stopped and where it started. There would be no guesswork involved, and nobody would get to vote on it. God Himself marked their territory, and He would expect them to uphold and defend the boundaries of it.

NUMBERS: Wisdom as You Worship

Read Numbers 34. Then, complete the sketch below to indicate where the cardinal boundaries of the Promised Land would be, per God's instructions.

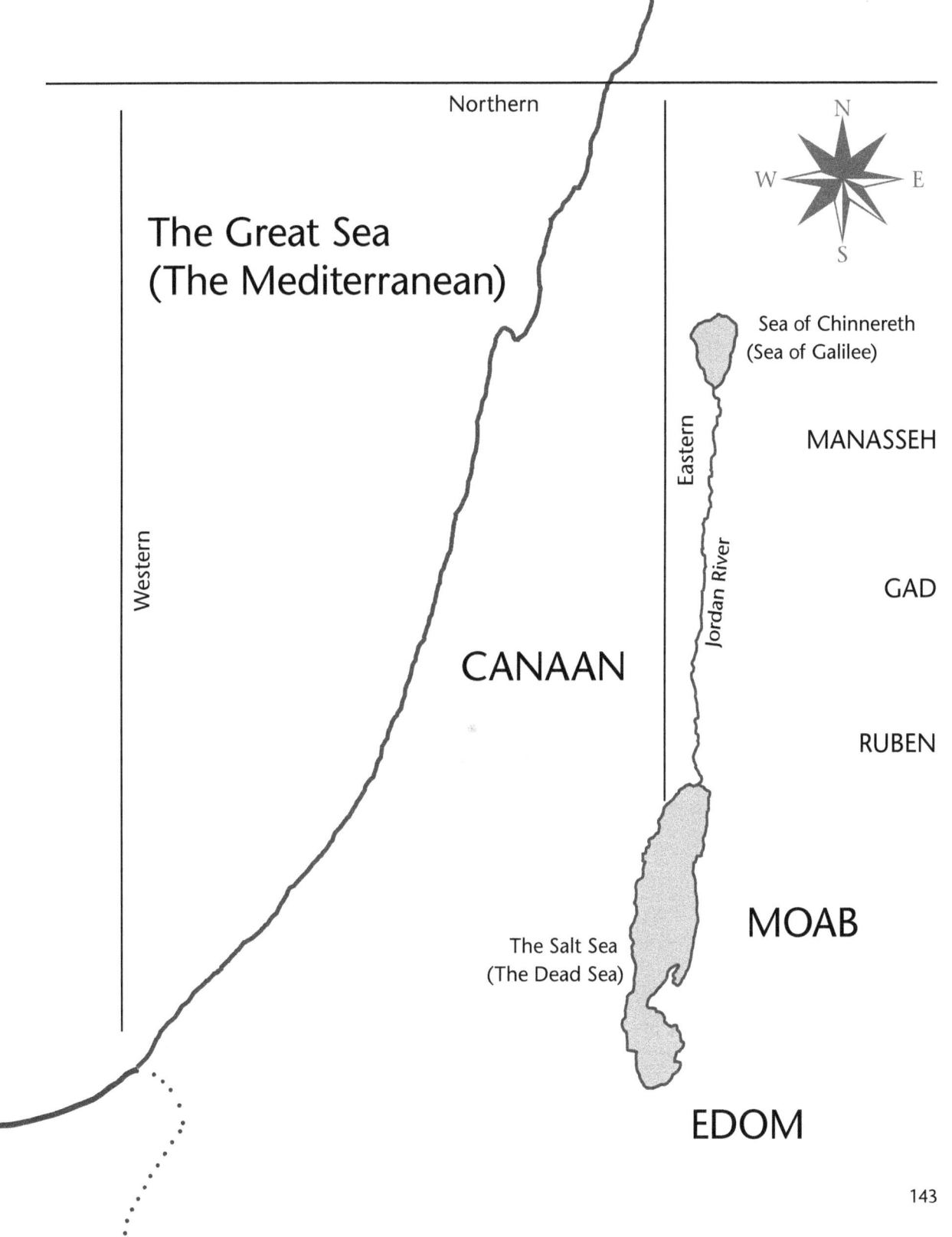

Chapter 13: *Leave an Inheritance*

Boundaries are funny things. We like them when they protect us, but we don't like them when they prevent us. The celebrated American poet Robert Frost contemplated boundaries in his poem "Mending Wall." He begins the poem, "Something there is that doesn't love a wall," and later adds, "that wants it down." The narrator's neighbor, however, insists that "'Good fences make good neighbors.'"

None of us would argue for the wisdom of property lines, but we may be a little less enthusiastic about the boundary lines God has set in place for righteous living. Though it may seem like this chapter was copied and pasted from a geography book or a Property Register's records, I think we can learn something here.

Notice that the boundaries were established **after** the Jordan. Only once God's people were in the land that He had prepared for them was their territory defined. As Christians, we tend to see symbolism in the crossing of the Jordan, as it hints at our transition from this world to our promised home of heaven. We should remember that there are boundary lines drawn for that inheritance.

I think we all know this, but let's repeat it anyway: Not all good people will be in heaven. Not everyone who sits in church on Sundays will be ushered into heaven's gates after Judgment Day. Not even all who are baptized into Christ will be there because, sadly, some will embrace sin and neglect the teachings of Jesus. Verses such as Matthew 7:21, 1 Corinthians 6:9-11, and Galatians 5:19-21 warn us of this.

So what are the boundaries for this inheritance? What gets us in and keeps us there? Let's look at Scripture's promises here.

Read John 3:5. What is a non-negotiable requirement for inheriting the kingdom of God?

_____

_____

Read Mark 10:17-31. What would have made a difference in a **good** man being a **saved** man, in this situation?

_____

_____

In the Sermon on the Mount (Matthew 5—7), Jesus begins by pointing out traits of those who will be in heaven. What are some of those traits?

_____

_____

Read Romans 8:13. Our eternal life is guaranteed if we live according to Whom? What does this involve, according to Paul's words here? (See also John 6:53.)

Read Matthew 12:50. What makes us family with God?

How do some people—even Christians—try to blur the boundary lines of the kingdom of heaven?

Part 2

Numbers 35

The email was an invitation to a cadaver lab session. As a faculty member on an extension campus of a Christian university, I was invited to attend a unique lesson in the School of Nursing one day.

Fascinated, I immediately made room in my day to attend. I confess that I typically follow true crime stories, and I am drawn to the intellectual challenge of solving the unsolvable, detecting the undetectable, and investigating the obscure. I further confess that's what motivated me to attend the cadaver lab. **A dead body or two. This is my chance!**

Though cadaver labs may be commonplace on large campuses, the opportunity to host one on a small extension campus was a privilege for the nursing students. The professor contextualized this medical opportunity as a sacred moment.

"From dust we were made, and to dust we return," he explained. "It's an honor that we do not take for granted to study the body designed by our Creator."

There was silence in the room for a moment, as we all stood around the sheet-covered corpse. The professor went on to explain that the woman we were about to examine had been a nurse. Training future nurses in the context of a Christian university was so important to her that she'd legally designated that her body be donated to this university for this purpose.

Chapter 13: *Leave an Inheritance*

I momentarily forgot about my interest in mortuary science. Instead, I was overwhelmed with emotion at what a selfless, brave choice this woman had made. Knowing her body would be stored indefinitely in a lab that countless unknown students (and curious professors from other departments) would examine her vulnerable, naked body and that she'd be quizzed over instead of wept over…she gave of herself.

And this is what I think of when I consider God's instructions to the Israelites. Let's read on.

Read Numbers 35. For what two purposes were the people of Israel to give of their land?

_____

_____

As a reminder of the nature of this land, what word does God use to refer to the land in verse 2?

_____

_____

What supportive role would the congregation play for a man in trouble (see verse 25)?

_____

_____

I read a lot. I enjoy most of what I read, but every now and then I read a book that haunts me. I call these "necessary reads" because they often contain uncomfortable truths that disturb my world and shake my comfort zone. I want this. I want to be shaken; I want to understand. I want to see. I want to hear.

But it hurts.

I recently read the story of Mexican immigrants whose perilous journey to the United States included many miles on *la bestia*, the cargo trains atop which migrants attempt to ride as they flee the violence of drug cartels in hopes of making it out of Mexico without being caught by the migration police, many of whom are on the payroll of the cartels.

When I finished this book, I grieved deeply for the humanity that has been lost in the political back-and-forth surrounding immigration to the United States. I have no answers, and I certainly won't politicize. I don't envy those whose job it is to mitigate these complex issues.

NUMBERS: Wisdom as You Worship

I will advocate, though, for the compassionate heart of Christ for those in trouble. I will advocate for the parts of ourselves that He calls us to give to those in need. For Israel, this looked like cities of refuge.

For us, Jesus was clear once again. Mark records Jesus' compassionate words to a very good, law-abiding man who obeyed the commandments. **Sell what you own. Give to the poor.** Matthew shares Jesus' explanation that we are serving Him when we give water to the thirsty and food to the hungry, visit those who are sick or in prison, clothe the naked, and provide shelter for strangers.

Before we dismiss Numbers 35 as ancient record, let's meditate on what Christ now calls us to do, with regard to helping those who are in trouble.

What are the hardest acts of benevolence for you to do, personally? Why are they hard for you? How can you become more practiced in serving God in these ways?

_____

_____

What keeps us from helping certain people? Is this biblical?

_____

_____

Who in your world could use some help this week? How can you help them?

_____

_____

What does Jesus say we must NOT do when we are performing good deeds? (See Matthew 6:1-4.)

_____

_____

Chapter 13: *Leave an Inheritance*

Part 3
Numbers 36

They hadn't yet inherited Canaan. They were in the plains of Moab, inching toward the Jordan. Yet God was already talking about boundaries and cities and inheritances. How exciting! I'm sure some of the younger Hebrews had the loyalty of U.S. Marines as they anticipated whatever combat necessary to claim the land they'd only heard about from their parents.

"**It's about to get real!**" one young man might have said to another soldier.

"**Let's do this!**" his comrade responds, as they both pace the ground, anxiously awaiting the call to arms.

There was likely sadness, though, among their parents. Probably reflecting on their sinfulness and grumbling of the past few decades, maybe some of them shed tears as they realized they would never get to enter the land their children would inherit.

One clan was particularly anxious. The land is real, even though they won't see it. But they want to make sure their stake in it is secure in future generations. Let's look at their concern in this final chapter of Numbers.

Read Numbers 36. What was the concern of the heads of the clan of Gilead?

_____

_____

According to the Lord's Word, how did Moses resolve this concern?

_____

_____

What was a general rule for each tribe's inheritance?

_____

_____

Did the daughters of Zelophehad obey?

_____

_____

NUMBERS: Wisdom as You Worship

I love the simplicity and beauty of verse 10: "The daughters of Zelophehad did as the Lord commanded Moses." I want to be this obedient! I want my legacy to be that I did as the Lord commanded—no more, no less.

God shared the people's concern in this chapter that His people keep their allotted inheritance. With ancient primogeniture laws ordering land to be passed down through male heirs, God arranges for each tribe's inheritance to remain secure even when there are no male heirs. His plan was simple: The daughters must marry within their father's tribe.

As we close the book of Numbers, let's ponder the instructions Paul gave to the Church, in terms of staying in fellowship with God.

Read 2 Corinthians 6:14-18. What are Christians told not to do?

Where do we see this teaching most often applied in the Church? To what other situations would this apply?

Why was this type of bond dangerous in the Church?

How do we resolve the need to be among the poor, the needy, the broken of this world, serving them as Christ would, YET still walk in obedience to this passage?

Chapter 13: *Leave an Inheritance*

Wisdom for Worship: Leaving an inheritance

Obeying the gospel gives us an eternal inheritance in the kingdom of God. But we are, at the very least, shortsighted if we see our Christianity as benefiting only us. A big part of our worship to God is our provision for those around us. Second Corinthians 4:7 reminds us that we possess a great **treasure**; we are but fragile **jars of clay**, just like every other person in this world. Every goodness in us comes from Christ, and if we love Him, we will keep His commandments to pass on the inheritance of His salvation.

There are immovable boundaries for our inheritance. We must stay within them. Why is it so easy for Christians to sin? More disturbingly, why is it so easy for us to try to justify our sin?

_____

_____

What are things you do to keep yourself from sinning? How can you share these strategies with your sisters in Christ?

_____

_____

Part of Christ in us is designated for those in need. How can you inspire more benevolence works in your own family? In your congregation?

_____

_____

What do you struggle to feel territorial about? From whom can you watch and learn—someone who gives and serves freely in this area of struggle for you?

_____

_____

Preserve the Church by building strong ties within it. Do your strongest relationships include Christians? Are there any relationships with Christians in your life that could be strengthened?

How do we guard against being too close to the world without being distant from the people in it (with whom we are called to share Jesus)?

www.ingramcontent.com/pod-product-compliance
Lightning Source LLC
Chambersburg PA
CBHW050749100426
42744CB00012BA/1943